1.54

THE LOWLAND INDIANS
OF AMAZONIA

PRINTED BY
WILSON'S PRINTING COMPANY, LTD.,
67b, TURNMILL STREET,
LONDON, E.C. 1.

Printed in Great Britain.

THE LOWLAND INDIANS OF AMAZONIA

A SURVEY OF THE LOCATION AND RELIGIOUS CONDITION
OF THE INDIANS OF COLOMBIA, VENEZUELA, THE GUIANAS,
ECUADOR, PERU, BRAZIL AND BOLIVIA.

With 14 *Maps.*

K. G. Grubb, F.R.G.S.

Heart of Amazonia Mission (World-wide Evangelization Crusade).

WORLD DOMINION PRESS

1, Tudor Street, London, E.C.4

1927

PRINTED IN GT. BRITAIN

FOREWORD

THE WORLD DOMINION SURVEY SERIES attempts to describe briefly and clearly the situation in various countries as viewed from the standpoint of the Kingdom of God.

The writer of this present survey, Mr. K. G. GRUBB, has made a very thorough study of the region dealt with here, and has extensively travelled in the Amazon Valley.

The problem of the lowland Indian is one of great difficulty for Governments, as well as Missions, and the situation is clearly set forth in these pages.

Some of the material has been printed in smaller type, as it does not make easy reading, but will be of special interest to the ethnologist and missionary.

ALEXANDER McLEISH,
Survey Editor.

LIST OF MISSIONARY SOCIETIES.

(a) *Societies working among the Lowland Indians.*

1. Assemblies of God (A.).
2. Christian and Missionary Alliance (C. and M.A., C.M.A.).
3. General Board of Foreign Missions of the Church of the Nazarene (C.N.).
4. Evangelical Union of South America (E.U.S.A.).
5. Gospel Missionary Union (G.M.U.).
6. Heart of Amazonia Mission : Worldwide Evangelization Crusade (H.A.M.).
7. Inland South America Missionary Union (I.S.A.M.U.).
8. Seventh-Day Adventist Denomination (S.D.A.).
9. Detroit (Michigan) Independent Mission (Ind.).

(b) *Other Societies mentioned in the Text.*

1. American Bible Society (A.B.S.).
2. Baptist Missionary Society (B.M.S.).
3. Bolivian Inland Mission (B.I.M.).
4. British and Foreign Bible Society (B.F.B.S.).
5. Canadian Baptist Foreign Mission Board (C.B.M.).
6. Christian Missions in Many Lands (C.M.M.L.).
7. Church Missionary Society (C.M.S.).
8. Foreign Mission Board of the Methodist Episcopal Church (M.E.Ch.).
9. Moravian Brethren (Missions-Direktion de Brüdergemeine) (Mor.).
10. Board of Foreign Missions of the Presbyterian Church in Canada (P.C.C.).
11. Domestic and Foreign Missionary Society of the Protestant Episcopal Church in the U.S.A. (P.E.).
12. Scandinavian Alliance Mission (S.A.M.).
13. Scripture Gift Mission (S.G.M.).
14. Society for the Promotion of Christian Knowledge (S.P.C.K.).
15. Society for the Propagation of the Gospel (S.P.G.).
16. South American Evangelical Mission (S.A.E.M.).
17. South American Missionary Society (S.A.M.S.).
18. Foreign Mission Board of the Southern Baptist Convention (S.B.C.).
19. Wesleyan Methodist Missionary Society (W.M.M.S.).

CONTENTS

APPENDICES.

INDEX.

MAPS.

INTRODUCTION

THIS Survey is an endeavour to describe the present condition of the Indian tribes of the region which it covers. The title does not denote its full scope, for it deals with the lowland Indians of Colombia, Venezuela, the Guianas, Brazil, Ecuador, Peru and Bolivia. The Andean peoples of the two latter Republics have also been dealt with. Only those parts of Bolivia and Brazil are discussed which lie north of parallel 18° S.—the southern limit of the Amazon basin. Thus defined, the area includes 4,085,000 square miles, or an extent of land slightly larger than the continent of Europe. It is primarily only the Indian population with which we are concerned.

Christian work among the lowland Indians of Amazonia is of such recent development that little reference can be made to converts and church organization. The Survey therefore deals with the people themselves. Those who are interested in the fauna, flora, industries and political and religious life of the various Republics should refer to the prolific literature already existing on these subjects.

On the regional maps Protestant Mission stations have been underlined, but further reference to the work of these Missions is confined to their relation to the problem of Indian evangelization.

A full discussion can be found of methods of approach, evangelism, education, agricultural work and other questions not treated here, in such reports as " Christian Work in South America," official report on the Congress . . . at Montevideo, Uruguay (April, 1925, 2 vols., 494 and 474 pages, New York).

Several previous surveys of the Indian question have been published, but I have not drawn on them to a sufficient extent to warrant their mention here. Acknowledgments are due to many who through correspondence or advice have contributed to adequacy of statement or accuracy of presentation.

The material for the Surveys is drawn from personal observation, from numerous published treatises of varying value, and from correspondence with missionary organizations.

It has not been thought necessary to note in every case the precise sources to which reference has been made. Such acknowledgments are, as a rule, therefore, introduced only when the actual words form the subject of a quotation. References are frequently written thus : 15 (1902) 805–12 = vol. 15 or XV., 1902, pp. 805–812.

It is necessary to draw attention to the great variety of spellings that from time to time have been adopted for the names of Indian tribes. For present purposes, with the exception of some names which are of outstanding familiarity, I have altered the spelling used locally to one which makes it more possible for English readers to pronounce these names. Those who are accustomed by residence on the field, or by the adoption of a particular phonetic system or by other ways to a different spelling, while they may not approve the present procedure, will doubtless recognize the difficulty of pleasing critics of opposing views.

K. G. GRUBB.

BIRKENHEAD,
    4th August, 1927.

The Lowland Indians of Amazonia

CHAPTER I.

Amazonia and its Peoples

I.

BEFORE dealing in particular with the various areas surveyed it is well to take a general view of this vast region. The mere contemplation of such a gigantic river-system as that of the Amazon-Orinoco cannot fail to impress one with a feeling of personal insignificance.

The Amazon is a prince among rivers, immense in its vastness and grim in the solitude of its wastes. Legend and imagination have invested it with a well-nigh impenetrable cloak of mystery. Yet its forests, so long the quintessence of the unapproachable, are rapidly yielding up their secrets to the explorer and the scientist. Ere long the last refuge of a persecuted race will be swept away before the irresistible advance of civilization.

The river rises in the Andes and flows into the Atlantic just south of the Equator. For more than 1,000 miles its course runs from south to north. The bend to the east is marked by the proximity of the Pongo de Manseriche where the waters burst through the mountain chain, and navigation in the plains below becomes a possibility. Three of its tributaries attain to 2,000 miles of length, ten more exceed 1,000 miles. To the north the waters of the upper Orinoco divide and send off a stream, 227 miles in length, to unite with her more powerful neighbour. This famous river, the Casiquiare, was discovered in 1744, and provides one of the most unique fluvial phenomena in the world.

The utility of many imposing streams is sadly impaired by the frequency of dangerous rapids. In ascending any of these rivers navigation is impossible beyond the first of these barriers. The tributaries of the south-western area, which rise in Peru, provide the most extensive stretch of unencumbered navigation, but in the neighbourhood of the lower river the navigable plain extends to little more than 100 miles on each side of the principal axis. Yet with all the inconveniences we have a remarkable area of navigable river surface. The main stream will float ocean liners at Iquitos, 2,000 miles from the Atlantic and only 500 miles in a straight line to the shores of the Pacific. The principal tributaries are highways for smaller river craft.

The cataracts of the tributary Madeira have been circumvented by a railway, and the heart of the Bolivian Republic has thus been made accessible.

The table in Appendix I. shows the principal tributaries and sub-tributaries encountered in a descent from the sources of the Marañon or Upper Amazon.

The important cities of the interior are few. Ciudad Bolivar (20,000), on the lower Orinoco, 240 miles from the mouth, is the metropolis of the inner regions of Venezuela. Pará (150,000), at the mouth of the Amazon, stands at the natural Brazilian outlet of the region. Manáos (40,000), a 1,000 miles further up, is the capital of the state of Amazonas, while the interests of Amazonian Peru centre in the river port of Iquitos (10,000).

This region first experienced commercial prosperity through the demand for rubber. Formerly the principal source of the world's supply was found in this favoured tropical garden. To-day the proportion is less than 10 per cent. In a momentous voyage the seed was gathered by Sir Henry Wickham, transferred to Kew, and subsequently transplanted to the Far East. The crude methods of extraction employed in the Amazon have never been able to resist the relentless competition of greater efficiency and the more permanent localization of the plantation yield. The blow fell in 1913-14. The price of rubber declined with startling rapidity. Scores of merchants were faced with bankruptcy. A chapter of industrial awakening closed in gloom and despair, and the dawning of a more prosperous day is still awaited.

As a result, numerous places which formerly were of some consequence are to-day deserted. The Brazilian population, attracted in the exhilarating days of the boom, is exhibiting an increasing tendency to return to their former homes in Ceará, from which many were originally driven by drought. The stimulus of the treasures of the forest had offered ample justification for a policy of wholesale devastation to minds to whom the Indian was a pariah and an inhuman beast. Hundreds had thus succumbed to the vandalism of their more powerful and so-called Christian neighbours. But the failure of the market so diminished returns that the risk to the trader could no longer be justified. Indeed, in the succession of these events, a discerning eye cannot fail to trace the intervention of divine justice.

To-day the principal industries are found in rubber, nuts, timber, and other products of the forest.

II.

The climate has been the subject of much undeserved abuse. The thermometer stands, on the average, day and night, at 81° at Manáos, and the annual rainfall of that locality is 65 inches. This temperature and precipitation compare favourably with West and Equatorial Africa, nor are the general climatic conditions in any way markedly inferior to those in the rubber growing region of Malaysia. Pará, however, receives nearly 100 inches, and west of Manáos there is another area of similar fall.

There are wide variations. Thus Porto Velho on the Madeira had 49 inches in 1914, and 153 inches in 1920. The seasons are two, " summer " and " winter," which have reference to the occurrence of rain and the rise and fall of the rivers, rather than to any difference of the thermometer. The main river and its southern tributaries rise in October-November and remain in flood till May, while in the northern basin and the valley of the Orinoco the seasons, when these phenomena occur, are reversed.

The diseases prevalent among the civilized population are attributable more to neglect and ignorance than to the actual unhealthiness of the territory. A recent medical commission reports : " The natives of Amazonia outside of the cities and towns live usually in small groups of palm-thatched huts, situated on the banks of the rivers or small streams, but occasionally located inland in the forests which have been cleared in their vicinity. The conditions of life in these settlements are most primitive. None of the houses are screened, nor are mosquito nets, except in very exceptional instances, used at night. The natives are exposed both night and day to the bites of all insect life. No hygienic measures are taken by the inhabitants of these localities in the disposal of excreta, the care or sterilization of drinking water, or other precautions against disease. There are no physicians and no drug or chemist stores outside of the cities. Generally speaking, the inhabitants living upon the river banks show evidence of either acute or chronic disease or the effects of having suffered from such disease. Portions of Amazonia to-day constitute some of the most unhealthy and most dangerous regions to reside in, from the standpoint of health, that exist in the tropics."*

---

* Strong, R. P., and others. Medical Report of the Hamilton Rice Seventh Expedition to the Amazon, in conjunction with the Department of Tropical Medicine of Harvard University. Cambridge (U.S.A.). 1926. 313 pp., p. 13.

III.

* TABLE SHOWING INDIAN POPULATIONS.

Region.	Area sq. miles.	(1) Population.	(2) Indian Population.	Percentage of (1) formed by (2)	Indian Population per sq. mile.
Colombia	441,000	5,855,000	117,000	2.00	.27
Venezuela	394,000	3,027,000	22,000	.73	.06
British Guiana ..	90,000	301,000	12,000	4.00	.13
Dutch Guiana (Surinam)	46,000	134,000	3,500	2.61	.08
French Guiana ..	24,000	55,000	1,400	2.55	.06
Ecuador (Andean section)	65,000	2,000,000	600,000	30.00	9.23
Ecuador (Lowland section) ..	55,000	80,000	25,000	31.25	.45
Peru (Andean section) ..	284,000	5,000,000	3,400,000	68.00	11.97
Peru (Lowland section)	250,000	200,000	71,000	35.50	.28
Brazil † ..	2,073,000	2,950,000	97,200	3.28	.05
Bolivia‡ (Andean section)	111,000	1,576,000	800,000	50.76	7.21
Bolivia‡ (Lowland section)	242,000	185,000	65,000	35.14	.27
Total (Andean sections)	460,000	8,576,000	4,800,000	55.96	10.43
„ (Lowland sections)	3,615,000	12,787,000	414,100	.32	.11
Grand Total ..	4,075,000	21,363,000	5,214,100	24.39	1.28

The above table needs a little explanation. The situation in Peru, Ecuador and Bolivia justifies the drawing of a distinction between such families as the Kichua and Aymara of the highland Andes and the Indians of the forest. The civilized Indians of Colombia and Venezuela, however, do not constitute a factor of sufficient weight to warrant such treatment, and

---

* This table absolutely supersedes any previous estimates which I have published. Considerable differences may be noted between these figures and those which I gave in *World Dominion* for April, 1927. (Grubb, K. G. " Amazonia and its Indian Tribes." *World Dominion*. London. 5 (1927) 184–190. p. 187.) Those figures were calculated from census reports and popular estimates. A totally different and infinitely more rigorous method has been followed in the present instance. The history and actual condition of each tribe has been examined according to the available information and a numerical allotment given to it. The totals thus obtained have been compared with official estimates from other sources and the results presented. The details of these figures will be found in the body of this work.

† Includes only the States of Amazonas, Pará, Maranhão, Goyaz, the Territorio do Acré, and part of the State of Matto Grosso.

‡ These two entries cover only the Departments of El Beni, La Paz, Cochabamba, Oruro, the Territorio de Colonias, and part of the Department of Santa Cruz.

consequently the entire population of these republics is included under the one heading. It is noticeable that the lowland Indians of Brazil are not, as is often supposed, the most numerous. It should not be assumed that this table conveys an exact representation of the condition of the Indians in the area. Such an analysis requires the consideration of a variety of additional factors. Many valuable deductions can, notwithstanding, be drawn from it.

A. Hay thus defines the term " Indian " : " By Indian, we mean people of the aboriginal race who retain their own language and customs. We include those who have come partially under the influence of civilization and Catholicism, but have preserved their Indian tongue, and can be effectively reached only in that language. We exclude such as are of Indian descent but have lost their original language and customs, having become virtually absorbed in the general population of the country."*

Many have found in this sparseness of population a justifiable disclaimer to missionary interest. The appeal of numbers is by no means to be despised. But the objection is far from being a novelty. It was urged with better discrimination when one of the greatest of our Societies was expending more money on the Indians of the Dominion of Canada than on the millions of China. The able Secretary of that period perceived in what direction the remedy lay : " There is therefore," he said, " clearly an obligation upon the Society . . . to take prompt measures to place these native converts upon a self-supporting system,"† but he added subsequently, " The Indians are now only the *remains* of nations ; but they are *living remains* ; and if it has been justly esteemed an enterprise worth much sacrifice of treasure and life to search through these very regions for the unburied bones of Franklin and his brave companions, surely

---

* Hay, Alex. Rattray. " The Evangelization of the Indians of South America." *Inland South America.* 20 (1925), 34–35, p. 35.

† Venn, Henry, in " Proceedings of the Church Missionary Society for Africa and the East." Sixtieth Year, 1858–9, London, p. 197.

the Church of Christ cannot refuse to send forth its messengers to search out, and to bring to life ever-lasting, remnants of tribes dead in trespasses and sins, yet inviting us by a living voice to go over and help them."* But if the Indian peoples demand much of Christian Missions they also have not failed to con-tribute towards the common progress. For the same authority is concerned to remind us of the extent to which news from the mission field among the Indians of the North-West was employed to provoke a zeal for the evangelistic enterprise as a whole. While at at a later period the distinguished historian of this Society remarks : " It used to be said that North-West America raised the funds which the C.M.S. spent in Asia and Africa."†

IV.

The physical characteristics, visible to the eye, which distinguish the Indian,‡ are the colour of the skin and the hair. The first is a warm, yellowish brown, sometimes inclining to red, but more often to bronze.

---

* Op. cit. Sixty-first Year, 1859–60, p. 215.

† Stock, Eugene. " The History of the Church Missionary Society." London. 3 vols, 1899, 504, 659 and 912 pp. Vol. IV., Supplementary Volume, 1916, 665 pp., p. 366.

‡ Numerous hypotheses have from time to time been formulated to account for the origin and presence in America of the Indian race. Some have considered that they represented the sons of Joktan of the line of Shem. Others have recognized them as the Hebrews and Tyrians of Solomon's fleets, and in 1869 de Thoron identified Ophir with the R. Japurá. It has also been suggested that here are to be found the Canaanites expelled from the Promised Land by Joshua ; while Lord Kingsborough published a treatise between 1831 and 1848 attempting to establish their identity with that of the Ten Tribes. This work, in ten volumes, cost him £32,000, and he died in 1837 in a debtor's prison. To-day the presence of the following racial elements has been established : (1) Australian ; (2) Malayo-polynesian ; (3) Asiatic (this is by far the most important, and to its permeation is to be attributed a uniformity of external appearance) ; (4) Uralian (the Eskimos). It need not be assumed that this list is complete, " Maya civilization, for example, seems to me to have a different origin " (Rivet, P, " Les Origines de l'homme Américain," L'Anthropologie. Paris. 35 (1925), 294–319, p. 311.)

The hair is long and straight, black and coarse, the skull either brachy- or dolicho-cephalic. The cranial capacity is superior to that of the negro but inferior to that of the white. The face is not strongly expressive and the lips are not thickened. The eyes are brown, or possibly black, small and oblique. The height is medium and sometimes great. In character we find the Indian impassive and patient, cunning and silent, and capable of great endurance.

Among the lowland tribes two definite types are clearly recognized. The distinguishing feature between them is the practice or non-practice of agriculture. In the first, economic and communal activities concentrate around processes of tilling the soil. These tribes form the large majority and enjoy a social pre-eminence, to the point of maintaining, in some localities, a degree of enslavement over their neighbours of the second group. The bulk of them adhere to extended linguistic families such as the Tupi, Arawak and Carib. They live in village communities under the control of a chief. Owing to the general lack of metal implements the forest is cleared with stone axes, while hunting and fishing supply them with a further source of food.

The non-agricultural tribes live entirely on hunting, fishing and the gathering of fruits. They correspond to the many units which remain to-day unaffiliated with any of the principal language groups. In eastern Brazil they are encountered (within the area of this survey) in a composite block stretching from the sources of the Xingú northwards, embracing the system of the Tocantins-Araguaya and portions of the States of Maranhão and Pará. Here they are termed Tapuyas, or more correctly Gê. All these tribes reveal a distinct inferiority of culture to the agricultural group. They do not use hammocks. With the exception of the Mura they mostly refrain from the manufacture of canoes. To-day, however, some have acquired methods of tillage from their white or Indian neighbours, but in many localities they are either disappearing or being absorbed.

Cannibalism of one form or another is still practised by certain tribes such as the Kashibo and the Parintintin. Head-hunting was characteristic of the Munduruků, and is still in vogue among the Jivaro of Ecuador. The blow-pipe is the weapon of a number of tribes, principally in the north-western region. Bark canoes are the usual means of travel. The double paddle has only been reported from two regions. The cotton hammock is chiefly characteristic of the Caribs and the Tupis, the palm-fibre of the Arawaks. Tattooing is widespread and lip-boring extensive. The ordeal of hair-removing is reported from every part. Games with india-rubber balls are the diversion of certain tribes. Pottery reveals little artistic progress. " It shows how conservative the Indian is towards anything that cannot make easier for him the struggle for life."*

Invisible forces, however, play the chief part in the life of the Indian. The substance of his relations to the invisible is found in animism. The dominant motive in his religion is evidenced in his fear of the human dead. Spirits are attributed to inanimate objects, to plants, to trees and to stones. Masked dances, magical ceremonies, the operations of the medicine man, ceremonial mutilations and numerous other ritual activities are essential to placate these mysterious beings. The distinction between the beneficence or the malignity of a spirit is not clearly drawn. The excellence of the origin of a demon affords no guarantee of the benevolence of his operations. The definite conception of the preternatural supremacy of a single deity is generally lacking. Indeed, missionaries have erroneously attributed deity to the spirits of national heroes, or to a being who appears, for example, to have partaken of a temporary prominence in, say, an act of creation.

---

* Nordenskiöld, E. " Comparative Ethnological Studies." " The changes in the Material Culture of Two Indian Tribes under the influence of new surroundings." Göteborg, 1920. 245 pp., p. 145.

V.

Among the important families of Amazonia, the Tupi-Guarani must be noted. Their ancestral home, where a great number are still found, was located in the republic of Paraguay. From here they migrated in different directions before the opening of the historical era. A division sought the Brazilian coast, dispersed along the littoral and finally penetrated up the Amazon more than 2,000 miles. They attained the Guianas in one direction and ascended the eastern members of the great tributary system of the south. Others, leaving their homes for the unknown tracts directly to the north of them, gained the upper courses of the Tapajos and Xingú. Others, again, moved west into Bolivia. Their propensity for travel by the water has earned them the title of the Phoenicians of America.

At this epoch the Caribs were established between the Upper Xingú and Tapajos. Under pressure from the south, they descended the southern rivers, crossed the Amazon and began to occupy the Guianas and Venezuela. Pushing northwards and possessing themselves of the coast, they drove before them the more pacific Arawaks and installed themselves in the valley of the Orinoco. From here they traversed the water to the West Indies, and even attained the coast of Florida. Others ascended the famous river till their proximity was realized on the Andean slopes of Colombia. The Caribs have always been an active and warlike people, exhibiting in times of peace an inclination for commerce and the contacts of trade. Humboldt has termed them the " Bokharians of the New World."

The Arawaks to-day are the most extensively scattered of all these families. They have been noted from Florida to Paraguay, and are distinguished more in the occupations of peace than in the arts of war. They appear to have migrated from the Negro-Orinoco region in a series of dispersions the sequence of which it is difficult to determine. Besides the regions mentioned, they were found in the West Indies, while the largest tribe is to-day established in Peru. They reached the Bolivian plateau and were there absorbed into the Inca empire, and are not encountered east of the Xingú.

It may be well to add a few words on the familiar topic of Inca civilization. Among the ancient Peruvians the governing community was the Inca state. The supreme authority was invested in a single ruler, whose power was absolute in all secular affairs. The people were organized in various divisions according to a well-ordered system for the purposes of administration. Labour was so systematized that the state could immediately summon able-bodied men for armed service or the prosecution of public works. The value of transport did not escape recognition, and military roads traversed the country from south to north. Religion demanded special worship devoted to the sun, whose representative upon earth was the Inca himself. In other directions they showed an equal degree of advancement. Agriculture was pursued with the aid of artificial irrigation. Metals were smelted, bronze manufactured from copper and tin, and stone and woodwork executed with a conspicuous degree of skill.

American Indian languages* are generally said to be characterized by features known as polysynthesis and incorporation. But in point of fact there are a number which do not share these indications. By way of illustration Boas points out : " In polysynthetic languages, a large number of distinct ideas are amalgamated by grammatical processes and form a single word, without any morphological distinction between the formal elements in the sentence and the contents of the sentence. . . . An example of what is meant by polysynthesis is given, for instance, in the following Eskimo word : takusariartorumagaluarnerpâ ? *Do you think he really intends to go to look after it ?* (takusar[pâ] he looks after it ; -iartor[poq] he goes to ; -uma[voq] he intends to ; -[g]aluar[poq] he does so—but ; -ner[poq] do you think he —; -â, interrogation, third person)."

---

* A list of linguistic families as far as our knowledge to-day permits classification will be found in Appendix IV. Reference should also be made to the maps.

" American languages have also been designated as incorporating languages, by which is meant a tendency to incorporate the object of a sentence, either nominal or pronominal, in the verbal expression. Examples of this tendency are the Mexican ni-petla-tsiwa. *I make mats* (petla-tl mat). . . ."

" A more thorough knowledge of the structure of many American languages shows that the general designation of all these languages as polysynthetic, and incorporating is not tenable."*

According to Rivet,† the multiplicity of languages recognized among the Indians of America is due to two causes. The first of these is to be found in the dissociation necessarily existing in a small population scattered over a vast area, and the second in the lack of any powerful civilizing language taking the place of the less important dialects.

Other interesting points in connection with Amerindian tongues cannot be enlarged upon here. Some of these concern such phenomena as the existence of distinct dialects for men and women respectively. Others exhibit peculiarities of diction and address such as are related in the experience of the celebrated missionary Barbrooke Grubb, who found it expected of him to address his remarks to a Lengua audience separately to the women and the men. Others, again, treat of the use of signs and communication by physical gesture.

The only language which was employed on an extensive scale as a "lingua franca" among the Indians of the lowlands was the Tupi. When the early missionary orders began work on the coast of Brazil, they speedily realised the serious disadvantages arising from a multiplicity of dialects. Adopting, therefore, the language mostly used among the Indians of the

---

* Boas, Franz. " Handbook of American Indian Languages." Smithsonian Institution, Bureau of American Ethnology, Bulletin No. 40, Pt. 1. Washington, 1911. 1069 pp., p. 74.

† Rivet, P. " Langues Américaines," in *Les Langues du Monde* by a group of linguists under the direction of A. Meillet and Marcel Cohen. Société de Linguistique de Paris. Collection Linguistique, Vol. XVI. Paris, 1924. pp. 597–712. Frequent use has been made of the numerous contributions of this author.

coast, they determined to press its acquirement on other tribes. To-day it persists on the River Negro, the Solimões and elsewhere, but is rapidly decreasing in importance. The language has been studied and grammars prepared but no portion of Scripture has been translated into it, the nearest approximation being the New Testament in the Guarani of Paraguay. The dialects of this " lingua geral," as it is called, differ slightly according to the locality.

It is commonly assumed that Indian languages vary considerably through the lapse of time and the vicissitudes of foreign relations. Whereas in general this is true, it is, however, not invariably the case. Commenting on different material in the Itonama language of Bolivia accruing at an interval of 100 years, Dr. Rivet remarks : " In the course of this long period, the language does not seem to have been modified in an outstanding manner, in spite of the particularly unfavourable conditions in which it has been transmitted. Spoken in a more and more restricted group of individuals, obliged more and more to have recourse to a strange language for all the exterior contacts of their life, Itonama has nevertheless preserved with remarkable fidelity its complicated grammatical structure."

" A more remarkable fact still is that its vocabulary is equally very little modified. . . . I have not noted greater differences between these words collected at an interval of a hundred years than those that one meets between vocabularies collected at the same epoch, but by different travellers. On the other hand, I have not gathered an abnormal number of words borrowed from neighbouring languages."[*]

An interesting comparison in this respect is emphasised in the Arawak Indians of Guiana, a locality also inhabited by a number of negroes originally imported from Africa. " The Indian borrowed from the European only the names of objects new to him, but the negro took many of the most commonplace terms, for which he must already have had proper equivalents. . . . This difference in the character of words taken by the negro and the Indian is not one of accident. It has a much deeper meaning. It demonstrates most convinc-

---

[*] Rivet, P.   " Nouvelle contribution á l'étude de la langue des Itonama. *Journal de la Société des Américanistes de Paris.* New Series. Paris. 13 (1921), 173–195, pp. 183–4.

ingly on the one hand the black man's ready response to new conditions, and on the other the red man's unyielding attitude."* Indian languages have even made contributions to European. Thus " cannibal " is a corruption of the name *Carib*, while *tabako* (tobacco), *hamaka* (hammock), *kanua* (canoe), and others are Arawak terms.

VI.

On May 30th, 1498, Columbus first saw the mainland of South America. In 1500 Cabral visited the coast of Brazil. In 1531 Pizarro invaded and conquered Peru. During the same year Ordaz ascended the Orinoco to the Meta and ten years afterwards Orellana descended the Amazon from the Andes to the sea.

The contact of the Indian population with civilization falls naturally into two sections : such contacts as came through the activities of the religious orders, and relationships established through the conflicts between the tribes and the colonists. The briefest reference only is possible here without referring to historical works in detail. On the eastern coast activities in the cause of religion commenced with the arrival of the Jesuits in 1549. Their early pioneers included many celebrated names, such as Vieira, Nobrega and the famous Anchieta, who, we are told, " won their hearts by his kindness and amazed them by his long prayers, his purity of life, his prophecies and his miraculous powers." The Carmelites landed in 1580, and the Benedictines a year later. In Peru, Portillo and seven Jesuits disembarked in 1568, while in the succeeding year they were followed by twelve new missionaries of whom " one, to the amazement of everyone, preached in the language of the Incas as soon as he came ashore. He had been studying it every moment of the long journey from

---

* Penard, Thomas E. and Arthur P. " European influence on the Arawak Language of Guiana." *De West Indische Gids*. The Hague. 8th Year. Aug., 1926, No. 4, pp. 165-176., p. 168.

Spain." In French Guiana, two Dominicans commenced in 1560, but were murdered on arrival. This was followed by the assassination of two Capuchins in 1643, while in 1639 four Jesuits had entered at another point. Such pioneers encountered great difficulties.

The colonists perpetrated the utmost cruelties among the Indians and executed the most inhuman massacres. In spite of the Papal Bull of 1537, which declared the Indians to be " real men," they even encouraged cannibalism in order to reduce the tribes to a speedy extinction. The method of the missionaries was to establish " reductions "* among the savages, a method which met with such success that the historian of Brazil† remarks, " So well had Nobrega and Anchieta trained their disciples that in the course of half a century all the tribes along the coast of Brazil, as far as the Portuguese settlements extended, were collected in villages under their superintendence." Church‡ quotes Fr. Gabriel Sala at a later date (1897) : " Among our Indians, not only of the sierras, but of the forests, one must bend their will even though it be by thrashing them with the lash, so that sooner or later they are taught and their understanding opens. This practice was followed in the time of the Viceroys, and is now the rule at some points on the Ucayali." On the treatment of the tribes by the settlers we read : " The Indians lived, deprived of their liberty without being masters of their wives or children, to serve everybody, irrespective of age or sex. Innumerable tribes perished, worn out in their efforts to satiate the avarice of the foreigner. The overseers also exploited them without remuneration, by augmenting their work. . . . Thus all of the tribes responded to the missionary fathers ' that Christianity for them was the surest

---

* The original meaning of this word, according to its derivation, contained the idea of " leading back " the savages from the wilderness.

† Robert Southey.

‡ Cited in Church, George Earl. " Aborigines of South America." London, 1912. 314 pp., p. 186. This work should be referred to for an account of the early relations of the Indians with civilization.

road to the loss of liberty and slavery to the Europeans.' "*

Since then civilizing agencies have sought to mitigate the danger of sudden contacts in many ways, but the prospect for the Indian is still gloomy. The spirit which made possible the persecution and brutality revealed recently on the Putumayo† is not yet dead. This subject will be referred to later. The Indian bears to-day the heavy burden of past contacts. Uncontrolled agents of commercial interests have indeed exploited him—violated the sanctuary of his forest dwelling, desecrated the intimacy of his family life, polluted his women, enslaved his children, razed his simple shelter to the ground, and left him to drain the embittered cup of remorse for a too sanguine and misplaced confidence. If this were all, some remedy might still be found, but disease carries away tens of thousands in the epidemics which have followed in the train of such contacts. Spreading with appalling swiftness, village after village will succumb without resistance till death reigns supreme over a countryside. A physician remarks : " It is above all to tuberculosis that the Indian race pays a tribute of enormous mortality. As these people have no idea of preventive hygiene, no notion of family contagion, they drink, healthy or sick, from the same calabash ; plunge their infected hands into the same plate of food, lie down several together in the same hammock, do, in a word, everything that is necessary for reciprocal contamination. By this system, the disease is spread with a frightful facility and some villages are at times decimated with an incredible rapidity."‡ Thus the final disintegration of the lowland Indian tribes seems at hand.

---

* Op. cit. Quotation from Las Casas on p. 227.

† Correspondence respecting the treatment of British Colonial Subjects and native Indians employed in the collection of rubber in the Putumayo District. London, H.M. Stationery Office, 1912. 165 pp.

‡ Tripot, J. " La Guyane. Au Pays de l'Or." Paris, 1910. 293 pp., p. 113.

VII.

As a matter of history, the presence of Protestants
among the Indians of the region should be dated from
1558, when a band of Huguenot colonists under
Villegagnon arrived at Rio de Janeiro, where they
found themselves in contact with the Tamoyo Indians.
The settlement was, however, early dispersed by the
Portuguese. For thirty years, from 1624 to 1654, the
Dutch were in Brazil, and at one time extended their
supremacy from the mouth of the São Francisco to
the state of Maranhão. They were frequently in touch
with the Indians. About 1664 Baron von Welz
attempted to rouse the Church of his day to a sense
of their missionary responsibilities. But meeting with
nothing but contumely and scorn, he sailed for Dutch
Guiana, where he found a martyr's grave*. The first
definite beginning of missionary work was that of
the Moravians in the same region in 1738. They
established themselves in the territory of the Arawak
Indians. In 1836 D. P. Kidder, of the Methodist Episcopal Church of U.S.A., travelled up the Amazon.
The latter part of the 19th century witnessed a re-
invigoration of Protestant Missionary enterprise.
In 1872 the South American Missionary Society
occupied Santarem, and in 1880 a launch was manned
for the equipment of an effort among the Ipuriná
of the Purus. After the drowning of a worker in the
first instance, and the expenditure of £10,000 in ten
years in the second, both these undertakings were
abandoned. In 1876, C. D. Dance, a missionary of
the Society for the Propagation of the Gospel, established temporary contact with the Chaima and
Warau of the delta region of the Orinoco. Later, in
eastern Brazil, the Krao were visited by Graham,
of the South American Evangelical Mission, and the
Gaviões by Witte, a missionary from the United
States. The latter subsequently attempted to initiate

---

* For an account of this remarkable man, see Pierson, Arthur T.
" The New Acts of the Apostles." London, 1914. 451 pp., pp. 74–7.

an enterprise on the upper River Branco among the Makushi. But in 1901 this was brought to a calamitous termination : " We had made very encouraging progress among them . . . when unfortunately an epidemic of fever broke out last year, which, along with many other Indians, took also my faithful companions, John Nounen and another brother, who, as a teacher, only joined our work last summer. Both were buried by the Indians, who later on carried me, half dead, to a friend's house down the river, whence in March of this year, I started for Europe to recover strength and find new fellow-labourers.

" A Canadian friend, Mr. Robert Phair, of Toronto, who, with his wife, was coming to our aid, landed in Georgetown (Demarara) on the same day when the others died. Robert bravely tried, when he found no news from us, to make his way with Indian guides to our station, only to find us gone, and he perished in the cataracts of the Essequibo on his way back.

" At present I am therefore alone, as far as human companionship goes. May it not be that someone at home may be led to say, ' Lord, here am I, send me.' "*

It is interesting to note that the S.P.G. have a work among these Indians to-day, and that their dialect is one of the few in which a Gospel has been translated.

In 1908, a deputation of the Baptist Missionary Society was despatched to Matto Grosso, having opportunities to visit the Paresi, Bororo and Tereno Indians. In 1909 Glass journeyed on the Araguaya among the Karajá, while the report of the conditions on the Putumayo resulted in the sending of two expeditions, but no regular work was established.

Since the war there has been a revival of interest in this whole region. It would be tedious to describe the journeys which agents of different societies have made during this time. I will, therefore, give a summary

---

* Witte, George R. " The Indians of Central and Northern Brazil." *Missionary Review of the World.* New York. New Series. 15 (1902), 805–12. pp. 811–12.

of the present situation as far as it is known to me, mentioning only work which is actually in progress among the lowland Indians.

Country.	Mission.	Tribe.	Locality.	Men.	Wives.	Date of Commencement.
Venezuela	Ind. ..	Piaroa ..	R. Parguasa ..	2	–	1923
Ecuador	G.M.U. ..	Jivaro ..	Oriente	1	1	1903
,, ..	C.M.A. ..	,, ...	,, (Tena) ..	1	1	1926
,, ..	,, ...	,, ...	,, (Macas) ..	2	2	1925
Peru ..	,, ...	Kampa ..	R. Pachitea-Pichis	3	–	1926
,, ..	S.D.A. ..	,, ...	R. Perené.. ..	–	–	—
,, ..	C.N. ..	Aguaruna (Jivaro) ..	North Peru ..	1	1	1925
Brazil ..	E.U.S.A.	Karajá ..	Bananal Island (R. Araguaya) ..	3	–	1924
,, ..	H.A.M. ..	Kayapo ..	R. Araguaya ..	2	1	1925
,, ..	,, ..	Krao	R. Tocantins (Carolina)	1	1	1924
,, ..	,, ..	Guajajara ..	R. Pindaré (Maranhão)	3	–	1926
,, ..	,, ..	Parintintin ..	R. Ipixuna (R. Madeira) ..	3	–	1925
,, ..	I.S.A.M.U.	Nyambikwara	Juruena (Matto Grosso)	2	2	1926
,, ..	A.	,, ..	Barão de Melgaço (Matto Grosso)..	2	2	1924

It is to be noted that only work actually in progress among the Indians is mentioned in the table. Other missions are represented in the area who either do not labour among the aboriginal population, or who, while contemplating such work, have not yet opened stations. In Pará and Manáos no less than five denominations are represented. It is evident that missionary work among the Indians, outside of the Guianas,* is of very recent growth. So far is this the case that it is still early to judge of the results. No reference, therefore, will be made to converts, even where such may exist. The Survey, as a whole, deals with entirely

---

* The work of the Missions in the Guianas is for the most part of longer standing and of a more settled character. It is therefore omitted here and discussed in the chapter on the Guianas. The location of Mission Stations is shown in the map of the Guianas.

virgin soil. Great as is the task which awaits accomplishment, this kindling of fresh interest is not a little gratifying. In a word, missions in this respect have struck their tents and are once more upon the march.

Hitherto the national churches in the republics of South America have taken little share in this work. There are, however, signs of increasing interest and a scheme has already been introduced in Brazil.* The Christian community in the republics and colonies discussed here amounts to 227,408, and in 1922 contributed £117,000† for the work of the Church. A negligible proportion of this, if any, can have benefited the lowland Indians.‡

VIII.

" South America," observes the Editorial Secretary of the Bible Society,§ " is the continent least represented on the Bible House Library shelves." The table in the Appendix shows that during one hundred years thirty-six translations have been published. These consist mainly of single Gospels and selections. The whole New Testament exists in two languages only, Kichua and Guarani. Most of the other languages in which translations exist are not known to missionaries to-day, and some of the versions also are out of print.

In addition, there exist various unpublished manuscripts. It will be observed that the three leading linguistic families of lowland Indians are included in

---

* For details, see p. 60 and " Christian Work in South America." Op. cit., Vol I., pp. 189–90, 192–5.

† " World Missionary Atlas." New York, 1925. p. 77.

‡ Roman Catholic Missions. A list of the missions of this Church constituted to work among the Indians can be found in Appendix III. It should not be assumed that these entries necessarily represent work actually in progress in the respective tribes.

§ Kilgour, Rev. R. " Bible Work in Central and South America," in " A Bird's-eye View of Latin America," *World Dominion Survey Series*, London. 44 pp., p. 21.

the table, the Tupi, the Carib and the Arawak. The whole New Testament exists in one of these only, the Tupi (Guarani).

Although the British and Foreign Bible Society have published versions in 593 languages of the world, among them the lowland Indian languages make only 1.5 per cent.

The American Bible Society carries on distribution of Scriptures in this area mainly through its Upper Andes Agency and its Brazil Agency. Naturally little has yet been done for the illiterate Indian. A Gospel or two exist in only seven of the four hundred dialects and languages used in the area under consideration.

The secretary of the Upper Andes Agency writes : " There are great stretches of territory that, because of the expense involved, are seldom or never visited by the Bible distributor. Then there are the Indian languages and dialects. Translations of the Gospels are urgently needed in these. . . . Two-thirds of the population is pure Indian, only seven per cent. white, and the rest is mixed blood." It is among the latter two classes that most of the Scriptures have been distributed. In 1926 in this area, including the whole of Brazil and Bolivia, over 400,000 Bibles, New Testaments and portions were sold. It is not too much to say that the work among the lowland Indians is still in its infancy.

The British and Foreign Bible Society appointed a sub-agent for the Amazon Valley in 1924. The workers of this Agency have penetrated to the borders of the Indian territory. The obstacles in reaching the Indians in their native languages are almost insurmountable. Apart from the fact that they are wholly illiterate, the few versions available in lowland Indian languages are only used in the Guianas and Paraguay. The others have fallen into disuse, and in very many cases the tribes are so small as hardly to justify the labour of translation. The solution of this difficulty will probably be found in the eventual acquisition by the Indians of Spanish or Portuguese.

IX.

Recent years have witnessed commendable efforts on the part of the governments concerned for the education and uplift of the Indians. In so far as they

affect Missions, these are noted under the separate
republics.   There is no question, however, that much
awaits to be done which can only be accomplished
by an efficient administration in the interior.   The
most remarkable of these projects is exemplified in
Brazil in the Indian Protection Service.   The work
which has been undertaken, though still in its initial
stages, cannot but win both the admiration and
sympathy of all who are interested in the prosperity
of the Indian race.   Though frequently hampered by
insufficient grants and compelled at times to employ
unsuitable agents, this department of the Government,
founded in 1910 through the initiative of General
Rondon, is a credit to the nation which has fostered
it and a greater honour to its celebrated founder than
a crowded life-time of military campaigns.   The Service
endorses the programme of José Bonifacio for the
Indian race, a programme which was based upon
justice, peaceful commerce, intermarriage, constancy
and endurance.   Article 219 of the regular instructions
reads thus : " It is not permissible for anyone in the
Service for the Protection of the Indians to avoid any
labour, any danger, any necessary sacrifice ; so that,
although the blood of many victims may have to be
freely shed by the dwellers of the forests, the sorrowful
remembrance of their four centuries of martyrdom
may be sufficient to inspire the true servants of this
great cause with fresh energy and fresh devotion."
   Whether the extensive establishment of reservations or localized colonies, as has been attempted
in Matto Grosso, would prove of the same value to
the Indians of Amazonia as it has to their North
American brothers is a question which is difficult to
decide.   As conditions stand at present the ultimate
future of the Red Indian of the lowlands, as distinct
from the agrarian communities of Peru, Bolivia and
elsewhere, lies in one of two directions : fusion with
the stronger elements or extinction.   The long, resist-
less years, coloured by unparalleled tragedy and
oppression, have ground the vivacity from the spirit
of the race.   Disintegration and dissolution have

succeeded the tyranny of conquering arms and strangled expectancy and hope. Disease and despoliation are the legacies of 400 years of atrocity and the sword. Civilization has offered to the Indian the offal from her marts and the sedge from off her foulest swamps and unwittingly he has accepted them as the bread of prosperity and the cup of peace. It sounds paradoxical to find, therefore, in the fusion of the two races the only solution of the present hour. Such a union produces a type of worker adapted to the country and combining many admirable qualities. The evils arising from this coalition are precisely those which the Christian Gospel should be best prepared to meet.

Missionaries to the lowland Indians contemplate with apprehension the history of a declining people, and realize that " when all is said and done our resemblances to the savage are still far more numerous than our differences from him."* To reach those who are yet alive with the message of their salvation is our task. To testify to our signal neglect in the past we may appeal to a witness once summoned upon a great occasion. At the conclusion of a speech of three and a half hours before the House of Commons, Wilberforce closed his arraignment of the inhuman traffic in Africa's flesh and blood by calling upon Death as his final witness, " whose infallible testimony to their unutterable wrongs can neither be purchased nor repelled." The great host has already passed on. Upon them the immense surprise of eternity has already broken. Already they are passed beyond the power of human ministrations. But if there is a sorrow more poignant than any for the dead, it is the sorrow for the living. " When He beheld the city He wept over it," and the tragedy of the past can only be redeemed by the rescue of what yet remains.

Primitive man is not devoid of uplifting aspirations. They move and stir in the depths of his spiritual nature. He has not refrained from identifying himself

---

* Frazer, Sir James George. " The Golden Bough : A Study in Magic and Religion." Abridged Edition. London, 1925. 756 pp., p. 264.

with his sacrifices and offerings. He has not hesitated to give the fruit of his body for the sin of his soul. In his inmost being he is touched by strange desires and provoked by impulsive questionings. But for all that he has not found peace. His way also is the yet unproclaimed way of the Cross, his Christ a Christ now hid from his eyes, the saving Companion of the forgotten and the despised, the afflicted and the oppressed.

CHAPTER II.

COLOMBIA

Area. Sq. miles.	(1) Population.	(2) Indian Population.	Percentage of (1) formed by (2).	Indian Pop. per sq. mile.
441,000	5,855,000	117,000	2.00	.27

Capital : Bogotá (166,000). Government : Republican under the control of a President elected for four years. Resources and products : Coffee, cotton, fruit, cattle, emeralds, platinum.

THERE is religious freedom in Colombia, but the Indians are under special laws. Thus by a decree of April, 1918, it was declared that " the Indians of the Uaupes are not subject to the common laws of the Republic, and will be governed ' en forma extraordinaria ' by the Missionaries charged with their reduction." Roman Catholic Missions in Colombia receive a subvention of 100,000 pesos from the Government.

The area principally inhabited by Indian tribes to-day is that which lies to the west of Long. 74° W. To this may be added the basin of the River Atrato and some isolated spots in the Andean and southern departments. The political divisions of the Republic and, in the north, the delimitation of its frontiers with Venezuela and Central America do not lend themselves conveniently to the discussion of the location of the tribes, but will be adhered to for other reasons. The Colombian census of 1918 returned the total number of Indians as 160,436. But no serious attempt was made to arrive at an accurate figure for those of the interior. For the description of these tribes we select four divisions* :

1. The northern area consisting of the Department of Magdalena and the Commissariat of Goajiro. 27,000 Indians.
2. The Andean Cordilleras. 12,000 Indians.
3. The Llanos. From the north-eastern frontier to the River Guaviare. 18,000 Indians.
4. The forest from the River Guaviare to the southern frontier. 60,000 Indians.

1. *The northern area, consisting of the Department of Magdalena and the Commissariat of Goajiro. 27,000 Indians.*

This area is prominent for two features : (*a*) The Sierra Nevada de Santa Marta, and (*b*) The Comisaria de La Goajira.

(*a*) The Sierra Nevada de Santa Marta presents a remarkable sight from the sea. Its intimate topography is still but little known, and it is a great attraction to explorers and travellers. Though often mistaken for the Andes by passengers bound for the coastal ports of northern Colombia, geologically it is not connected with that range. The mountainous massif must be regarded as an outlying prolongation of the Antilles land mass, whose main axis lies east and west, in contrast to the north and south extension of the Pacific cordilleras.

The Sierra is inhabited by the *Aruak*, who are members of the Chibcha family. Actually they are divided into four groups, of which the principal is the *Kágaba* on the northern slope of the Sierra in the villages of San Antonio, San Miguel, Santa Rosa and Pueblo Viejo, and in San José on the southern slopes. The Bintukua, the Guamaka and the Atankez are also on the latter slopes.

A peaceful and docile people, the Aruak have always shown loyalty to the government. A repudiation of any indulgence in commercial relations outside the tribe is accom-

---

* These divisions are shown in Key Map inset on Map of Colombia, p. 35.

panied by a disinclination to afford the customary hospitality to strangers.

A few chapels signalize the presence of Christianity in their midst, but the visits of priests are rare and the people maintain a number of their customs intact without infringement. Both Spanish and their own dialect are spoken. Access to the region by boat is readily assured from Santa Marta or Riohacha, an inconsiderable interval alone separating the former from Barranquilla. The nearest Mission Station is in Santa Marta, where the Protestant Episcopal Church of the United States is represented. Maracaibo is not far distant, but is in Venezuelan territory.

(b) The Commissariat of Goajiro or Comisaria de La Goajira.

This is the most northern portion of the mainland of South America. Between it and the Department of Magdalena, the River Rancheria, with the small town of Riohacha at its mouth, has provided a convenient boundary. The peninsula itself lies north-east and south-west. The traveller may advance through the south-western area to a small distance beyond the Teta mountain, traversing in this section an extensive and fertile plain. The north-eastern half presents a volcanic conglomeration of hills. These are indicated by three parallel ranges about 2,000 feet in height crossing the peninsula from north-west to south-east.

The whole of this region is inhabited by the *Goajiro*. Popular estimates have attributed to them 80,000 souls, but the actual number need not be assumed to exceed 25,000. Their affiliation with the Arawak family is clearly demonstrable from their language. To-day they must be one of the largest tribes in the entire region under consideration in this survey. Their frontier, owing to international disputes, is watched by Colombia and Venezuela alike. Within their territory they reign supreme. In contrast to the Aruaks, they are a vigorous and warlike people, constantly breaking out amongst themselves. They are divided into about thirty clans, of which the most important are the Uriana and the Epieyue, while the

Kosina, living in the Cojoro Hills and the Teta, are the most belligerent. The remainder are encountered chiefly between the mountains and the coast, while a few at Sinamaica have pile dwellings in the shallows of the Gulf of Maracaibo.

It is extremely desirable that something should be accomplished speedily for this fine nation, for it is a question how long they will be able to withstand the perils of commercial contact. The Spanish Capuchins established a mission among them in 1888. Their work is limited to two orphanages, one at San Antonio on the north bank of the River Rancheria, and the other at Nazaret, at the base of Mt. Itajoro in an attractive section of the Macuire Hills. The nearest Protestant Mission station is at Maracaibo (120,000) in Venezuelan territory (see p. 58). Some of the Goajiros, who have acquired Spanish in addition to their own dialect, appear there frequently for trade, and Sinamaica, where a few are found, is on the Venezuelan side of the frontier. Apart from this approach, they are reached from the same ports referred to when discussing the Aruak.

A remnant of the *Chimilá*, descendants of the former Tairona (Chibcha), lives in the neighbourhood of the River Ariguani, a sub-tributary of the Magdalena.

2.   The *Andean Cordilleras*.   12,000 Indians.

In the first historic days of Colombia's discovery, the Andes were populated by a number of tribes, all belonging to the Chibcha family. They had attained to a marked degree of civilization, falling short, however, of the achievements of the Aztecs and the Incas. Although feuds and divisions were common amongst them, they built towns and villages, promoted extensive trading expeditions, and pursued agriculture. They enjoyed the use of metals, and must have possessed a great quantity of gold. Their worship was accompanied by human immolation and centred around certain sacred and famous lakes. To-day we have only a few disjointed remnants of this race, one or two of which have already been mentioned. Others, probably in considerable numbers, are so merged in the general population that we cannot distinguish them here. In most cases there remain but a reduced number of pure-blooded Indians, and the smaller tribes are in danger of disappearing. The following notes include all the existing sections in Colombia. The Aruak and Chimilá have already been referred to.

The *Guatuso* are established on the River Frio, a southern affluent of the San Juan, on the contiguous boundaries of the Department of Valle and the Intendencia of Choco, with a few survivors on the Rivers Cucaracha, Guacalito, Sapote and the estuary Boca Negra.

The official Indian population of the Department of Boyacá is returned as 5,308. The composition of this population is mainly derived from the *Tunebo* Indians. The region they occupy is generally known as " Tierra Adentro," and, like most of the areas occupied by the Indians, is far removed from the beaten track. Precisely delimited it covers the slopes of the Eastern Cordillera for over a hundred miles from the sources of the Arauca to the northern affluents of the Meta, and the western slope of the Cordillera of Cocuy. Their sub-tribes bear various names, dwelling on the streams of similar denominations. Of these it is only necessary to mention the Pedraza, who prefer the San Lorenzo, a left-affluent of the Margua, and the Nula. They are the only savage section. On the right bank of the Margua are found some Tunebo, whose dialect and customs are very different from those of the Cordillera of Cocuy.

On the whole the Tunebo are comparative strangers to the evils of modern civilization. Their houses, which are oblong, are difficult of identification, and they are mistrustful of the advances of the white man. In 1923 they were still in a rudimentary state of progress, making their fires with two pieces of wood and showing little difference in culture from their neighbours of the deeper forests. It is estimated that at the discovery they could be computed at 6,000. To-day some estimates attribute to them 4,000–5,000, but precision demands an allocation of some 3,000. They have been attacked by epidemics of late, and reduced in numbers. The Eudists or Missionary Priests of Jesus and Mary, have, within the last few years, attempted to start work among them.

In the Department of Cauca there are a few remnants of different tribes, although the census of 1918 returned only 438 for Indian population of this Department.

The *Paez* originally lived in thirty-four villages between the upper Cauca and Magdalena. Tradition has endowed them with the distinction of cannibalism, and even to-day they are somewhat distrustful of the Colombians. A very few *Panikitá* still remain in the village of that name in the same region. In addition we find remnants of the *Totoro*, *Moguex*, *Kokunuko* and *Guanaka*, originally sub-tribes of the Paez. The last representatives of the *Andaki* are located at the sources of the two rivers Fragua. The first of these flows direct into the Caquetá, a left-affluent of the Amazon. The second, by the intermediation of the Pescado, throws its waters into the Orteguasa, a left-affluent of the Caquetá.

In the Department of Nariño, near the small village of Altaquer, lives an extremely interesting people, the *Kwaiker*. Their habitat is in the valley of the River Vega and on the left bank of the Guabo, which it joins, as far as Altaquer, but on the opposite bank. The Guabo, or Güisa, is an affluent of the Mira, which forms a small sector of the boundary between Colombia and Ecuador. While living peacefully they preserve a strict exclusiveness from the outside world. In 1918 they numbered about 600. The Curé visits them once a year to celebrate all the feasts of the Church since his last visit. Thus " at certain times one can attend in these farms in the course of a week, the Corpus, Nochebuena, Holy Week, All Souls' Day, etc. In this journey the Curé . . . did not finish with any more feasts than those of Nuestra Senõra de las Lojas, Santa Barbara, San Rafael, San Sebastian, Santa Rita and the Crucifixion."[*]   The Kwaiker are a Chibcha tribe belonging to the same group as the Kolorado and Kayapa in Ecuador. It is rare that a woman speaks Spanish, but the men have usually an acquaintance with that language.

The *Telembi*, of whom there are a few on the Patía, belong to the same group. The *Yumbo* live to the east of Pimampiro in Ecuador.

This completes the list of Chibcha tribes surviving to-day in Colombia. The list originally included over fifty names, but of these many survive only in the chronicles of the past. Except among the Aruak, the Tunebo and the Kwaiker, the Chibcha language in this republic is to-day, for all practical purposes, a language of the dead. For the rest, these Indians either speak Spanish or Kichua. The employment of the Kiteño dialect of the latter tongue is to-day confined to the south of the republic, the Department of Tolima and the

---

[*] Gutierrez, Rufino. " Monografias." Bogotá. 1 (1920), 153–6.

Andaki Indians. The introduction and extensive propagation of the language of the Incas as of common utility, is, of course, of comparatively recent date and due to the influence of the early missionaries. Even at the end of the 16th century catechisms and ecclesiastical documents were still being produced in the different tribal dialects. The settlement of Spanish-speaking Indians at San Andres in the Department of Bolivar is typical of many other such settlements spread over the country.

There are Protestant Mission stations in this area at Bucaramanga, Bogotá, Medellin, Palmira, and Cali, while during 1925 the Christian and Missionary Alliance occupied Popayan and Ipiales in the south.

In addition we have to mention several tribes which, while falling within the geographical limits of region (2), do not belong to the Chibcha family.

The first of these is the *Mokoa*. Koché, their language, is only now spoken by the last representatives of this people, who, in 1907, numbered 500, in the village of Sibundoy, on the extreme upper Putumayo, where they are delivered to the charge of a Spanish Capuchin missionary. The language, of which only four words are known to us, has nothing beyond a history interest, as to-day they speak Kichua.

The *Chokó* Indians inhabit the Intendencia of that name. It is characterized by the River Atrato, which flows into the Atlantic, but whose sources so nearly attain the waters of the Pacific. The Indians, some of whom live in a wild and untutored state, are found in the basin of this river and on the Pacific coast between Lat. 4° and 8° N., a forest region. The identity of a large number of sub-tribes which it would be tedious to refer to here has been established, and the sites of their villages are generally found on the affluents of the Atrato. They number perhaps 5,000.

The Chokó was originally occupied by the Franciscans. It forms an apostolic prefecture which was handed over in 1908 by the Sacred Congregation for the Propagation of the Faith to the Sons of the Immaculate Heart of Mary. Very little, however, has been done for the Indians in any direction. In 1915 some nuns of the Carmelites of the Diocese of Antioquia visited the less familiar villages and reported a promising response to their advances. It was proposed to constitute an Order for the prosecution of the work, but I am unaware of the subsequent history of this attempt. The nearest Protestant Mission is at Medellin, the second city of the republic, with 90,000 inhabitants, where the Board of Foreign Missions of the Presbyterian Church of the United States maintains a station founded in 1911.

Finally mention is demanded of the Indians of the Opon and Carare. These rivers are affluents of the right bank of the Magdalena in the Department of Santander. The Indians, who are known only by these names, are encountered in the forests on their banks. They are hostile and a serious menace to the safety of travellers passing through their country. They belong to the Carib family, but their number is unknown.

3. *The Llanos.*   18,000 Indians.

This area includes that stretch of land which lies east of the Cordillera Oriental of the Andes and west of the River Orinoco, which here marks the frontier between Colombia and Venezuela. Its northern and southern limits are coincident respectively with the north-eastern political boundary and the River Guaviare, or Guayabero, the greatest of the affluents of the Orinoco and which some hold to be the true source of that celebrated river.   The region in its entirety consists of a vast expansive plain, reaching out, if viewed from an altitude, to a horizon of the evenness of the ocean.   Coarse, tall grass is the characteristic vegetation, interspersed here and there by oases of palms and belts of trees. Countless streams, some insignificant brooks and others navigable for large craft, flash across the plain.   The rivers are confined between walls of forest, and in the winter the floods encroach upon the lower land.

The principal tributaries from north to south are the Arauca (480 miles), the Meta (660), the Vichada and the Guaviare (810), all of which flow approximately east to join the Orinoco. Politically the region is divided, somewhat arbitrally, into one Intendencia, that of the Meta, and two Commissariats, of Arauca and Vichada.   The Indian tribes belong in the main to the Guahibo and the Arawak families.

The region is very inaccessible and travelling is hard. The Meta enters the Orinoco in its navigable reaches below the

Atures rapids. Occasionally it is visited by steamers from Bolivar, the metropolis of the lower river in Venezuelan territory, which ascend to Orocué, 300 miles from the confluence. The mails from Bogotá to Arauca, a customs town of 4,000 inhabitants on the frontier and capital of the Commissariat, travel by way of Orocué and take forty days. Villavicencio on the upper Meta is two and a half days from Bogotá, and from here the upper courses of the Vichada and Guaviare are difficult of access.

The following tribes represent the Arawak family in this area : The *Achagua* and the *Tamude* may still have a few representatives in the region. The former live not far above Orocué, on the Ele, Casanare and other affluents of the upper Meta, and the latter on the River Ele. They both speak Spanish. The *Amorua* are found in the neighbourhood of the Rivers Tomo and Tuparo, between the lower Meta and the Vichada. The *Amarizama*, possibly to the number of 1,000, occupy the banks of the lake and Rivers Uva and the Aguas Blancas, left-affluents of the Guaviare. The *Chukuna*, a small tribe, are said to exist near the sources of the Manacacia and the Vichada. The *Mitua* are reported near the left bank of the Guaviare, below the confluence of the Ariari, probably in the neighbourhood of the lake Mapiripan, although the small settlement of Mituas was formerly on the lower Uva. By far the most important Arawak tribe of the region is the *Piapoko*, who live on the middle Guaviare, principally between the confluence of the Ariari and that of the Uva. They seem to be the descendants of the former Kabre (a tribe who infested the entire Guaviare from its mouth to the Ariari, and were well known to the early religious orders). They may number about 3,000.

The bulk of the Indian population of this region is composed of the elements provided by the *Guahibo*. The census of 1918 gives the joint Indian figure for the Intendencia of Meta and the Commissariat of the Vichada at 27,400. Although this seems considerably in excess of the real number to-day, the principal contributors to the total must be the Guahibo, who are usually quoted at 15,000–20,000. Even such a moderate estimate would appear generous.

The following tribes are known to exist : the *Guahibo*, properly so-called, between the Meta and Uva and particularly on the River Vichada, and they are occasionally seen north of the Meta ; the *Kuiva*, Mella or Ptamo in the hinterland of the right bank of the lower Meta ; the *Chirikoa* on the Lipa and Ele ; the *Katarro* on the Yucabo ; the *Kuiloto* on the River Cravo. These latter are left-affluents of the upper Meta. The *Yamu* dwell on the left bank of the lower Ariari, two days' canoe journey from the mouth, and the *Churroya* on the main stream of the River Guaviare above the confluence of the Ariari.

The Guahibo belong to the class of Indians referred to on p. 17–19 as non-agricultural. They tend to be nomadic. The Yamu, however, whose linguistic connection with the Guahibo has yet to be demonstrated, and who are a river people, boast of both houses and plantations inland from the river. They have, in common with all the Guahibo, a reputation for being treacherous and unreliable. The Guahibo proper are sometimes encountered on the cattle ranches of the Meta. However, a propensity for raiding civilized settlements must be considered among their characteristics. The Vichada and the Muco are as much frequented by them as any streams of the district. The family is linguistically an independent one.

The tribe was never successfully approached by the early missionaries, and their instability and intractable disposition were the despair of many a zealous Father. " The Guahibo have been the testing-stone of our former and modern missionaries : the crucible where their patience and suffering have been refined, and a field which, after cultivation with incredible toils and watered also with the sweat and tears of many labourers, has shown itself barren, dry, and ungrateful, and in place of corresponding fruit has produced nothing but spines and weeds ; a generation of gipsies, or a branch of them, who are delivered over to a vagabond life to whom every fixed place, even though full of conveniences, appears an intolerable prison and the insupportable oar of a galley."*

No work has been attempted among these people. There has been a revival here, as in many regions, of

* Gumilla, José. " El Orinoco ilustrado. Historia natural, civil, y geographica, de este Gran Rio." Madrid, 1741. 580 pp., p. 191.

the endeavours of the preaching orders of the Church of Rome. The Augustinian Recollets commenced in 1893 a " Mission to the Heathen " in the locality of the River Casanare, which was constituted an apostolic vicariat in the same year. No definite attempt has been made to reach the wilder Indians, and the few that have been in touch with the mission have benefited little by the contact.

The nearest Protestant Mission station is in Bogotá, the capital, although another small mission, with its home office in Detroit, has recently been initiated on the River Parguasa, a right-affluent of the Orinoco (see p. 64), in Venezuelan territory.

The *Sáliba* are to-day reduced to a few remnants encountered on the River Meta, and possibly on the Vichada, the total numbering not more than a 100.

A small number of *Piaroa* live on the left bank of the Orinoco and its affluents the Zama and Mataveni (see p. 63). These two tribes, the Sáliba and Piaroa, form the principal constituents of the independent Sáliba linguistic family.

4. *The forest from the River Guaviare to the southern frontier.** 60,000 Indians.

This region has been but slightly explored. Particularly does this remark apply to the immense area stretching from the sources of the Caiary-Uaupes, considered by some to be the main stream of the River Negro, to the Andes, which is doubtless inhabited by tribes of which nothing has been hitherto reported. There are serious obstacles to exploration, especially in the rainy season. Paths which are at all in regular use then become chains of swamps, bogs and marshes. The forest is traversed by several ranges of hills, alternating with profound ravines in which torrential streams race downwards to the river plain. Game is readily scared away. Insects are plentiful and insistent. Occasionally the monotony is interrupted by areas of bush land with a tangled, contorted mass of coarse

---

* The frontier with Ecuador and Peru is still in dispute. In this section are discussed all the tribes as far south as the Napo. For the Putumayo region, see p. 54 and 82.

lower growth, even more difficult to negotiate than the denser jungle itself.

From the Andean plateau of Colombia the region is accessible by descending to Villavicencio and working south through San Martin across the Guaviare to Calamar, a small rubber port on the upper Uaupes, now, however, in a state of abandon. This is an extremely fatiguing journey, the conveyance of any sort of cargo incomparably increasing the problem of transport. In lieu of this route the Inirida can be ascended from San Fernando de Atabapo, or the Guainia, Isana and Uaupes by working up the River Negro from Manáos through Brazilian territory. Such are the impediments that these rivers present in their innumerable rapids that upstream navigation is excessively laborious. This is pointedly true of the Uaupes. Towards the south the Caquetá (called in Brazil the Japurá) provides a means of access. Parts of the upper course are broken by hazardous falls, but free navigation extends from its confluence with the Amazon, 450 miles to the mouth of the Apaporis, a river whose sources are in the heart of the area under review. The Tolima-Huila-Caquetá railway is planned to extend from Espinal on the Tolima Railway to Neiva, and thence south to the head of navigation on the upper Caquetá. About forty miles of this extension have been constructed to date (1926), and the completion of the enterprise would materially contribute to the accessibility and prosperity of the region. But to render the Caquetá navigable throughout its length demands an engineering scheme of considerable ambition, including the circumvention of the rapid of Araraquara, 860 miles from the mouth, where the river drops about 100 feet.

In this wilderness of forest the most important tribe is the great group of the *Umawa*, commonly recognized by the Colombians as Karijona. They live from the sources of the River Apaporis west to the River Yary or de los Engaños, another left-affluent of the Caquetá. From here they extend to the River Orteguasa, thus distributing themselves over a vast territory between Long. 72° and 76° W. Substantial numbers are often given, and Whiffen mentions the figure of 25,000.* The correct estimate seems considerably less than this, although it is certain that they are tolerably prolific.

The following sub-tribes are known : the *Hianakoto* on the River Macaya, an affluent of the upper Apaporis, and the Cunyary, a sub-tributary of the Yary. The *Tsahátsaha* south of the former on the Cunyary and Mesaya, affluents of the Yary. The *Mahotoyana* on the River Macaya. The *Karijona* on the source-affluents of the Yary with a few families on the Caquetá, and a short distance above Puerto Cordoba some individuals in an agricultural colony, together with a few Witoto, Miranya, and Yukuna Indians under Colombian direction. At Puerto Cordoba itself there dwells a young man, a son of a Colombian and a Karijona Indian, who was educated at Fribourg in Switzerland. Although speaking French he has lived among his tribe on the upper Yary and married a Karijona woman. The *Yakaoyana* are found on the Apaporis. The *Kaikutshana* are neighbours of the Kauyari (Arawak) who live on the Pirá-paraná and other affluents of the Apaporis. The *Kahätonari* live on the River Mesaya ; the *Guaké*, an important group, on the River Yary and a part of the Caguan and Orteguasa.

The Umawa or Karijona exhibit but small dialectical differences among themselves. They are members of the great Carib family, being the most westerly offshoot of that family at present found in South America. According to their own traditions and from other evidence they must have migrated to their present location from the Guianas as a consequence of their contact with the whites. Many are still in a savage and untutored state. The vagueness of this information is a defect consequent upon the inaccessibility of their country. To pass from the Caquetá to Bogotá (the capital) involves an exhausting journey of sixty days in wild country. This journey, if concluded by, say, a descent of one of the great western affluents of the Orinoco, would constitute an invaluable enterprise of missionary reconnaissance. The route to Bogotá is only followed by Colombians of the Caquetá when expense prevents the round journey by the Amazon and the Atlantic.

The principal neighbours of the Umawa on the east

* Whiffen, T. " The North-West Amazons." London, 1915. 314 pp., p. 59.

are the *Tukano* tribes. The Tukano family is not encountered east of the Negro-Orinoco, or south of the Amazon itself. It is, therefore, comparatively localized, and of the number of such families found north of the central river, it is the most widespread, if, to-day, it cannot attain to the place of numerical pre-eminence.

The Tukanos fall conveniently into three geographical divisions : (*a*) A northern group falling within region (3) and found at the sources of the Manacacia, an affluent of the Meta. This consists of the Tama and the Airiko, but both tribes are probably now extinct. (*b*) The western group found principally in south-western Colombia with some representatives in the adjacent zone of Ecuador. (*c*) The eastern group in Colombia and Brazil occupying principally the right-affluents of the upper River Negro and the River Apaporis.

Judged by this last group, the Tukano have shown themselves to be a powerful and enterprising people. Appreciative of the strength and advantages of co-operative effort, they have exhibited a tendency to aggregation resulting in the establishment of powerful communal villages. They whole-heartedly devote their time to the pursuit of agriculture, planting mandioca, maize, sugar-cane and numerous varieties of fruits. Their handiwork witnesses to a laudable degree of skill and dexterity, and as pilots of the dangerous rapids they manifest the most enviable coolness, the result of habitual familiarity with the rivers from the earliest boyhood. The chief holds his office by hereditary right, and possesses considerable influence and power. His reputation, however, is often rivalled by that of the medicine-man. To him is attributed an occult sovereignty over things intangible and invisible, and control of bodily diseases is held to lie within his power as much as the vagaries of rain and storm. Ceremonies of a magical and religious character, to join in which the Indians will gather from considerable distances, are a feature of their social life. They centre round the cult of " Jurupary," a deity who, in his origin, seems to have been beneficent, but who has undoubtedly acquired a sinister and evil reputation.

Passing over the first group of these Indians, the following tribes belong to (b) :—

The *Tama* and *Koreguaje* live in two villages, Puikini and Mekasarama, consisting of five communal huts on the Orteguasa. They are still comparatively untouched by modern civilization. The *Makaguaje* live in similar simplicity between the upper Putumayo and the Caquetá, on the Caucaya, a left-affluent of the former and the Mecaya and Sensella, right-affluents of the latter. They are not numerous. The *Siona* live at San José on the right bank of the upper Putumayo below the confluence of the Guamués. They are a small tribe speaking Spanish and their own dialect of Tukano.

The Spanish conquerors applied the name " Enkabellado " to a group of the Indians they encountered on the Napo. Their true name is *Pioje*, and they are still known in small numbers between the Aguarico and the Napo and the latter river and the Putumayo. Some of them are established in the civilized settlements of the Napo together with the Zaparos. The list of their sub-tribes formerly known extends to eighteen names. The *Abijira*, strictly speaking, belong to Ecuadorean territory. They live between the Napo and the Curaray, and, according to some Ecuadorean travellers, further down the Napo between the Curiyacu and the Mazan. They are to-day probably included among the savage Indians known as Aukas, a considerable section of whom belong to the Zaparo family. The Abijiras have always been considered hostile.

This completes the mention of the western group of Tukano tribes existing to-day whose total number may be considered as 1,500. A list of their tribes and sub-tribes recognized by former pioneers includes 100 names.

Group (c). The Eastern Group. The tribes of this region are often briefly referred to as the Uaupes Indians. They trace their connection, however, to different units, all of which have suffered through contact with civilization. Geographically, they are divided between (i.) the River Uaupes, the principal right-affluent of the River Negro and its tributaries ; and (ii.) the River Apaporis, a left-affluent of the Caquetá. These two systems are, however, intercommunicable by various routes employed by the Indians.

(i.) Colombian territory on the Uaupes includes all the upper river. The middle course forms the boundary with Brazil, continued along the River Papuri, a right-affluent, and then passing south so as to include nearly all the course of the Apaporis. Working from west to east, or descending the

D

river, the following tribes are encountered : the *Hölöwa*, at the sources of the Cuduiary and Querary, left-affluents of the Uaupes.   Originally Arawak, they have been absorbed by the Tukanos.   The whites know them as Baniwa, a confusing term applied to different groups of Indians.   On the Querary they are also known as Yulämawa.   The *Kobewa*, who include the Koroa, Bahuna, etc., are found on both banks of the Uaupes and on the Papuri, a right-affluent.   The *Wanana* are also found in small numbers on the middle Uaupes.   They number, perhaps, 100 to 200 souls.

On the River Papuri, a right-affluent of the Uaupes, there are representatives of a number of tribes, including the Tukano, Desana, Waikana, Tuyuka, or Doghapura, Tariana, Siglia, Wanana, Kobewa, Karapaná, Diria, Waínana, Bariguda, Kawiria and Pamóa. The Indian population of the river perhaps amounts to 5,000, of whom a 1,000 are Tukanos and 500 Desanas who will be mentioned when discussing the adjacent area of Brazil.

These Indians of the Papuri, for the most part, preserve their own dialects, which are all of Tukano family. The Tukano, as spoken by the tribe of that name, serves as a "lingua franca" among all the Indians on the river. It does not, however, command a sufficiently extensive acceptation to justify its classification as the language of commercial relations or as of value for the instruction of other groups. Those who speak it are adjudged the possessors of a symbol of unmistakable superiority over their less intelligent neighbours. As a whole the Indians of the Papuri are a degenerate people, only doing the minimum necessary to support their daily needs. Bestiality and immorality of the coarsest nature are common among them, in contrast to other groups. Disease is rampant. Their normal span of existence can hardly exceed forty years, and they are rapidly dying out.

Father Kok, of the Society of Mary, with its principal centre at San Martin, in the Llanos of Region (3), is in charge of a mission among them, and at its stations on the river, San Bernardo and San Huberto, some 200 Indians, principally Desanas and Tukanos can be encountered. This priest published (1920) in the *Eco d'Oriente*, a Colombian paper, Tukano texts of the Lord's Prayer, Ave Maria, the "Commandments of God and the Church" and a number of prayers and forms of ritual. While at Villavicencio he printed vocabularies of 2,000 words in six languages: "lingua geral" (Tupi), Tukano, Desana, Waikana, Tuyuka and Makú, with the minor catechisms in the same languages and in the "lingua geral," and in Tukano a collection of hymns and a grammatical sketch.

The Indians of Tukano family of (ii.), the section of the River Apaporis, may be sketched as follows :—

The *Bará* live at the sources of the Tikié, a right-affluent of the River Negro. Their habitat places them close to the Apaporis and within easy communication with that system. They are extremely primitive people, related linguistically to the Tuyuka. The *Yupua*, very few in number, are found to the south of the upper Tikié, and on the upper Oocá, a left-affluent of the lower Apaporis. The *Buhágana* is the name of a group comprising a number of sub-tribes of which the names and identities of some eight are known to me. They dwell on the Pirá-paraná, a left-tributary of the Apaporis, and its affluents on both banks, the Dyi, Tariira and Yauacaca. The Apaporis, which, owing to the difficulties involved in its navigation, still lacks a thorough exploration, has been already mentioned in connection with the important tribe Umawa or Karijona, and furnishes, in addition, a refuge for the following small Tukano groups, naming them as they are encountered in an ascent from the Caquetá :—

The *Yabahana* live on the Weki-paraná, a right-affluent. The *Opaina* are divided into sub-tribes of which the most important are the Letuana and the Tanimuka. The former live one day's journey above the Pirá-paraná ; on the Cupeya, a right-affluent of the latter three days further up ; on the Pama, also a right-affluent. Five days' ascent of the river from this confluence, all navigation ceases at the falls of Yanicoera, which are said to be higher than Niagara, but of which competent observers have hitherto brought no account. The *Yahuna* are hidden between the Apaporis and the Mirití-paraná, another and less important left-affluent of the Caquetá which flows parallel to the Apaporis and enters the main stream some sixty miles above it.

Although a few miles on the Brazilian side of the boundary we may mention here a colony of twenty-two civilized Indians on the Japurá (or Caquetá), a short distance above the mouth of the Puré, a right-affluent, which is composed of individuals from the Tanimuka, Kueretú and Makú tribes, together with one Yukuna and one Yahuna.

A few *Yuri*, an independent family, may still be existing on the Puré.

The Tukano tribes thus enumerated in Colombian territory number probably not more than 8,000.

The Puináve family is represented in Colombia by the following tribes in region (4) :—

The *Puináve* or Epined of the River Inirida, a right-affluent of the Guaviare, entering that river close to the Venezuelan frontier town of San Fernando de Atabapo. They are inferior to the tribes of the Uaupes, both in handiwork and in social organization. Among themselves and towards other tribes they are friendly and honest, though their negotiations with the traders of San Fernando are usually fraught with discontent or bloodshed, due largely to the trader's utter disregard of customs which are precious to the Indian. Their canoes are exceedingly small, and one man can readily take one from the water and cache it in some hiding-place in the forest.

The *Makú*, of whom it will be necessary to say more when discussing the tribes of north-west Brazil, live scattered amongst the Tukano tribes, who often enslave them, and are encountered between the upper Uaupes and its affluents the Papuri and the Querary.

The Arawak family is not without its representatives in region (4). Apart from some outlying tribes, such of them as have escaped extinction live on the Atabapo, a tributary of the Orinoco, the Guainia or upper River Negro, the Isana, a western affluent of the River Negro, and the already discussed Caiary-Uaupes. The Atabapo and the lower Guainia mark the frontier between Venezuela and Colombia.

The *Yavitero* live in the little village of Yavita on the upper Atabapo, strictly speaking, in Venezuelan territory. The survivors speak a conglomerate of various Arawak dialects and Spanish. The *Baniwa* were once, and still are, the principal tribe of the Guainia. They live in a number of small villages on the Guainia, at Maroa on that river, along the course of the Atabapo, and intermingled with the population of San Fernando. To-day there are only 100 souls in Maroa and Yavita together, and the total number of Baniwa perhaps attains to 150. They are a capable, intelligent and peace-loving people. But their beautiful women could not escape the unbridled lust of the civilized inhabitants of these distant regions, with the consequence that there are now very few pure-blooded Indians surviving. Of the *Warekena*, formerly a ruling tribe, feared and hated by the whites, there are a few representatives on the Guainia and on the Atabapo.

The Indians of the Isana, who are all Arawaks, perhaps number 1,500 souls. The white population applies the name " Baniwa " to them, but actually several different tribes are represented, employing differing dialects. Occasionally a mixed village is encountered, but normally it is a perquisite of these small groups to preserve a serious aloofness from their neighbours of the adjacent locality, which finds a recurrent relaxation only for some ceremonial visit of importance, or when circumstances throw them together in the unwilling service of the white man. From time to time a frenzied religious festival will attract a company drawn from the villages of many days' journey in all directions. The Indians of the Isana are polygamous.

The following are the principal tribes working downstream from the sources :—

The *Kuati* or Kapiti-minanei live at the sources and on the left bank of the Isana and as far north as the Papunaua, a right-affluent of the Inirida, which, by a short portage affords communication between the two rivers. The *Tapiira* dwell on the Surubí-paraná. The *Payoarini*, above the Ipeka on the Arara-paraná, a left-affluent. The *Ipéka* or Kumatá-minanei : their chief village is Santa Barbara on the main river, but they are also found on the Yavareté-paraná, a right-affluent. The *Siusi* among themselves rejoice in the name of Oalíperi-dakeni. They are distributed in three sections : (*a*) on the lower Cuiary, an important left-affluent of the Isana ; (*b*) on the middle Aiary, a big right-affluent ; and (*c*) on the Isana from above the big rapids to the mouth of the Aiary. The Moliweni of the lower Cuiary are a sub-tribe of (*c*). The *Adzaneni* or Tatú-tapuyo occupy the upper Cuiary, the upper Guainia and affluents of the latter, such as the Tomo, Aquio, Naquieni and others. On the lower Aiary dwells a rougher type of Indian, with features very different from the finer appearance of the Siusi. They are the *Huhuteni*, who have a tradition of having spoken a strange language, only adopting the Arawak more recently. The chief inhabitants of the Aiary are the *Kawa*.

Separated from the Indians of the Isana by the group of Tukanos, which we have already discussed, we find the *Kauyari* (Arawak) who wandered from the Isana and now occupy the Cananary, a left-affluent of the Apaporis and the Pirá-paraná, on which they are known as the Wainamby-tapuyo. A few *Yukuna* Indians, of whom the Matapy are a sub-tribe, are found together with other Indians in the civilized establishments of the Caquetá (see p. 51). The remainder of this tribe, now much reduced in number, lives between the Mirití-paraná and the Apaporis.

This concludes the list of the Arawak tribes of Colombia.

Owing to the confusion and diversity of dialects obtaining among the Indians of the eastern portion of region (4), it may be useful to emphasize the fact that communication is here fairly easy. The principal languages spoken are :—

(1) Tukano. Among the tribes of that family. The various dialects are all mutually intelligible.

(2) Arawak. On the Guainia Spanish-Arawak patois is employed. On the Isana pure Arawak.

(3) Lingua Geral or Tupi. (See p. 22–23.) This is fast dying out. It is still in force on the Isana, the Uaupes and the upper Rio Negro. It is rapidly being replaced by (4) or (5).

(4) Spanish. Among many of the Indians of the Guainia, upper Rio Negro, Inirida and parts of the Isana and Uaupes.

(5) Portuguese. Among the more intelligent Indians of those parts of the River Negro basin which fall within Brazilian territory.

(6) Other dialects are used such as Makú, which is rapidly disappearing owing to the absorption of this people by stronger nations. Karijona, a Carib dialect, is spoken throughout that important tribe which has very little contact with civilization.

It is not uncommon to encounter a Tukano or Desana Indian of the lower Uaupes who can make himself intelligible in no less than four languages, Tukano, Lingua Geral, Spanish and Portuguese.

Finally, it is necessary to mention the *Witoto* (Huitoto). These Indians live, it is said, to the number of 20,000 on the Orteguasa, referred to on p. 49. Their centre is in the village of Niña Maria. They are the Indians who formerly occupied the Putumayo territory (see p. 82). Consequent upon the cruelties to which they were then subjected, they migrated into Colombian ground. Here they still preserve their original customs and employ their native language, which must be considered as forming an independent family.

Protestant Missions in region (4) are non-existent. Popayan and Ipiales in the Departments of Cauca and Nariño are occupied by the Christian and Missionary Alliance, and it is, therefore, the nearest mission to this area. Manáos, in Brazilian territory at the confluence of the Rivers Negro and Amazon, is a station of the Southern Baptist Convention (Richmond), and a centre for the Heart of Amazonia

Mission (but see also p. 96). To travel between Ipiales and Manáos by the River Caquetá-Japura is to cover a distance of 2,000 miles without encountering a mission station or the merest indication of Protestant work with the exception of some Brazilian Christians on the banks of the Amazon above Manáos.

The Capuchin Mission in the village of Sibundoy at the sources of the Caquetá has been referred to under region (2). (See p. 41.) In region (4) the only Romanist mission at work is that directed by Father Kok on the Papuri, the details of which are given on p. 50.

In Colombia, as elsewhere, the era of prosperity for the native Indian race has long since passed. The tribes we have reviewed in these brief notes form but the skeleton of a former population. The flesh and the bones, the sinews and the life-blood, are already dried up. A noted traveller in region (4) remarks : " The sores inflicted by the destroying locusts, who are traders in rubber, but slaughterers of men, have spread. The hard work in the fever-stricken forests, violence, ill-treatment, and murder must have carried off thousands of Indians . . . happy in their life without ambitions, because they are still ignorant of the value of gold, now besides their natural failures, they only learn the vices of European civilization, alcohol, syphilis, the power of money and other diseases. Blood and destruction follow the track of the white man in America."*

---

* Koch-Grünberg, Th. " Zwei Jahre unter den Indianern." 2 vols. Stuttgart, 1909–10.

CHAPTER III.

VENEZUELA

Area. Sq. miles.	(1) Population.	(2) Indian Population.	Percentage of (1) formed by (2).	Indian Pop. per sq. mile.
394,000	3,027,000	22,000	.73	.06

Capital : Caracas (135,000). Government : Republican based upon elective and representative principles. The present constitution was sanctioned in 1922. President holds office for seven years. Missions in Venezuela among the Indians are subject to a Law of Missions. This enacts the appointment of a Director approved by the Government, the establishment of primary and agricultural education, the debarment by authority of undesirable persons from the territory, and the provision by the Government of the expenses of the undertaking.

Resources and products : Coffee, cacao, sugar, stock-raising, balata, oil. British capital invested in Venezuela : over £10,000,000.

IN this discussion of the Indians of Venezuela we propose to observe three geographical divisions:

(1) The State of Zulia and the Maracaibo region. 5,000 Indians.

(2) The region north of and on the left bank of the lower Orinoco and the Indians of the delta. 3,000 Indians.

(3) The right-affluents of the Orinoco, the state of Bolivar and the Department of Amazonas. 14,000 Indians.

VENEZUELA

0   100   200   300
English   Miles

LINGUISTIC FAMILIES.

Arawak   Carib

Saliba   Others

Geographical Names Maroa   Tribal Names   Yaruro

World Dominion Press.

KEY-MAP
Figures refer to
divisions in text.

2
3

45

SUCRE

Carúpano
Río Caribe
Barcelona
Cumaná

NDA

Maturín
Guanipa

ANZOATEGUI

MONAGAS

Unare

CO

Guato

R. Orinoco

Bolívar

Caroni

El Callao
Guasipati

Cuyuni

B O L I V A R

Caura

Guanare
Taparito

Yahuana

Manchuri

Yaharana

Caroni

Paragua

Mt. Roraima

5

Arekuna

RORIO
ritorio

Meveyari

Katiuna
Auaris

NAS

Guainia

Uraricuera

Esmeralda

Umao

Siapa

Branco

10

TEARITORIO
DELTA AMACURO

Warau

60

65

60

H.G.Grubb.

(1) *The State of Zulia and the Maracaibo region.* 5,000
     Indians.

The chief geographical feature of this region is that
remarkable arm of the sea, the Gulf of Maracaibo,
but it is not on this that the most important tribe is
found. The *Motilon* prefer the refuge of the Sierra de
Perijá.

The Sierra de Perijá contributes to the boundary
between Colombia and Venezuela, the actual frontier
being considered to follow the line of highest altitude.
Exploration hitherto has penetrated to but a limited
extent. The last few years have seen a revival of
scientific enquiry into the oil industry of Maracaibo.
The mountains offer many difficulties, even to a thoroughly equipped expedition. The trail which was
formerly supposed to have connected the Colombian
and Venezuelan sides of the watershed is now legendary.
The lower slopes of the mountains are heavily forested,
and the successive spurs are divided by precipitous
ravines through which pour a series of torrents which
eventually reach the Lago de Maracaibo on the
Venezuelan side and the Magdalena on the Colombian.

The *Motilon* live largely in Colombian territory,
but as commercial interest in the region has found a
convenient centre in Maraciabo, we have considered
them from the Venezuelan side. Formerly they
occupied the environs of the Colombian villages of
Cucuta, Ocaña and Catatumbo. Their migration to
the higher ground is of comparatively recent date.
They are divided into a number of tribes, of which the
following are the principal :—

The *Yukuri* are found on the western slopes of the Sierra
in the neighbourhood of Socomba and the upper Maracá.
The *Chaké* are divided into various sections ; the *Makoa*
dwell on the Venezuelan side on the River Apon near the white
settlement of Machiques. Other groups of which some bear
the names of local rivers, include the *Apon*, *Aponcito*, *Rio
Negro*, *Pariri* and *Yasa*, and occupy the upper River Negro.
The *Tukuku* are reported on the river of that name, an affluent
of the Santa Ana. The *Chaparro* and *Irapeno* are established
further to the south. On the Rio de Oro, a left-affluent of the
Catatumbo, additional groups may be also encountered.

The Motilon are a hostile nation. The Colombian sections are more disposed to friendly relations than the Venezuelan. On the upper Negro and Santa Ana they can only be approached through the mediation of the Tukuku, of whom a few speak Spanish, and are employed in a farm near Machiques on the Aponcito. Culturally and linguistically they belong to the Carib family, but there is no doubt that they have been profoundly modified by the influence of their environment. They have large fields, but no domestic animals. They use no salt, and have only recently acquired the use of matches. Their villages are mostly at an altitude of some 4,000 feet, and access to them is a toilsome task. They consist of small settlements of a dozen or more huts. Their total number is about 5,000, among whom there are a number of albinos.

It is earnestly to be desired that something be done immediately for this people, who would probably best be reached through the Tukukus of Machiques. It is unlikely that they will resist, for any length of time, the pressure and encroachments of civilization. There are already some twenty oil companies working the Maracaibo region, and heavily armed expeditions have been commissioned to explore the Sierra de Perijá. The southern Motilon are accessible from Encontradas, an oil centre of 2,000 people on the lower Catatumbo, which is in steamer communication with Maracaibo.

On the Colombian side there is a Roman Catholic mission carried on by a Spanish priest at La Grange. The nearest Protestant Mission station is in Maracaibo, a port of 120,000 people, where the Scandinavian Alliance Mission of North America is represented. Some of the Motilon Indians live within fifty miles of Maracaibo.

The *Goajiro* have been discussed under Colombia. As the boundary is now delimited, the bulk of the tribe is in Colombian territory. In the south-eastern part of their domain they extend, however, into Venezuelan ground, where their principal centre is the village of Sinamaica on the Gulf of Maracaibo. A sub-tribe of the Goajiros, the Parauhano, are established to the number of 100 in the villages of Sinamaica, Santa Rosa and El Mojan, with a few representatives on the island of Zapara.

(2) *The region north of and on the left bank of the River Orinoco and the Indians of the delta.* 3,000 Indians.

The very sparse Indian population of this region includes only a handful of pure-blood Indians.

The remnants of four tribes are found in the State of Lara. A few individuals of the *Ayaman* dwell in the suburbs of the municipios of San Miguel, Aguada Grande and Moraturo ; the *Gayon* in the municipio of Bobare ; the *Jirajara* in the environs of Siquisique ; the *Ajagua*, neighbours of the Jirajara on the north. These few Indians all speak Spanish to-day. The linguistic material at our disposal in their dialect does not justify a union with any other linguistic family.

The last survivors of the *Karib*, a tribe of the Carib family, are found in a part of the State of Monagas and the southern part of the State of Anzoátegui, as far west as the rivers Unare and Suata, where they are being rapidly absorbed by the white race. A few are known south of the Orinoco.

The delta of the Orinoco and north-western section of British Guiana are occupied by the *Warau* or Guarauno. The entertaining fiction that their natural shelters were in the branches of the trees has long since been exploded. Their canoes constitute their principal title to fame. With remarkable dexterity they construct them from a single log of cedar fifty or sixty feet long and five or six feet in breadth. Naturally dark in hue, their dirty habits give them an even duskier appearance. They attain, perhaps, the number of 3,000. Their language has not been successfully affiliated with any other, and must therefore be regarded as independent. In the delta of the Orinoco many speak Spanish.

The *Yaruro* (independent) occupy the Capanaparo, a left-affluent of the Orinoco, numbering perhaps 200 souls.

(3) *The right-affluents of the Orinoco, the State of Bolivar and the Department of Amazonas.* 14,000 Indians.

The sources of the Orinoco are as yet unreached. The upper river is remarkable for its connection with the system of the Amazon. The Casiquiare canal, a natural waterway, unites the two, carrying the water of the Orinoco to the upper River Negro. The canal,

according to Rice,* is 281 feet above sea-level at the
Orinoco, and 212 feet at the Negro end, while at the
latter confluence it is 2,150 feet broad. Its economic
value, however, is entirely destroyed by its inaccessibility and the occurrence of numerous rapids. Esmeralda is the highest civilized settlement. San Fernando
de Atabapo stands at its confluence with the Atabapo,
Inirida and Guaviare, and not far below the mouth of
the Ventuari. Below this spot communication is more
frequent, but the river is interrupted by dangerous
falls, in particular those of Atures and Maipures. The
affluents of the upper Orinoco drain much unexplored
territory. Steamers ascend the main stream occasionally
to the mouth of the Meta, that affluent and the Apure
both being navigable for considerable distances. Ciudad
Bolivar, a place of 20,000 people, is the centre of the
river trade. It is situated at the narrows some 240
miles from the mouth, and is in direct communication
with Trinidad.

The Indians of this region belong principally to
the Carib, Arawak and Piaroa families. They live on
the far upper Orinoco and on the remote courses of
its affluents, with an increasing tendency to retreat
to the more distant regions under the mountains,
where their tribal activities and mutual relations
may suffer less from the relentless interference of
modern commerce. We will, therefore, initiate their
description by dealing with the forests of the headwaters of the principal river and its tributaries.

The lower river is the recipient of the outflow of two streams
which run from south to north, rising in the Sierra Pacaraima,
the frontier between Brazil and Venezuela. They are the Caroni
and the Caura. The *Arekuna* (Jarikuna) live partly in British
Guiana, and are also seen in Brazil. Conspicuously handsome
forest Indians of the Carib family, in Venezuela they occupy the
upper Caroni and its left-affluent, the Paragua, to the vicinity
of the Caura. The *Makiritaré* stretch from the Auari to the
Orinoco. The former is an extreme source-affluent, in Brazilian

---

* Rice, A. Hamilton. " The Rio Negro, the Casiquiare Canal, and
the Upper Orinoco, September, 1919–April, 1920." *The Geographical
Journal*. London. 58 (1921), 321–44, pp. 329, 335.

territory, of the Uraricuera, belonging to the Amazon system. They are found on the Merevari, as the upper Caura is termed, on the left-affluents of the Ventuari, and right-affluents of the Orinoco, the Padamo, the Uapó, and the Cunucunuma. They are divided into a number of sub-tribes, which are shown on the map. Their largest village is probably that known as San Remo, near the source of the Padamo, two days' overland from Esmeralda. Singular interest attaches to these people, who are now in the twilight of their history, and whose memorials are full of the pathos of the disastrous results of contact with civilized man. Once a proud and warlike nation, they were also the foremost merchants of the Caribs of the hinterland. On the Caura they were known as Waiomgomos, the tribe which credulity and mendacious report induced Raleigh to describe as the headless men. They total perhaps 1,000 souls or more. The *Yabarana* (Carib), who were once the chief nation of the Ventuari, are now reduced to some twenty individuals, who live on the River Manapiare, a river which enters the Ventuari on the right bank about 170 miles from its mouth. The *Kurasikana* are reported to be very hostile. They occupy the Bishita, a source-affluent of the Suapuré, a right-tributary of the middle Orinoco, as well as the upper Manapiare. The *Vökiare*, or Guaykiaros, are peaceful. They are established at the sources of the Parú or Paré, a right-affluent of the Manapiare. These two Carib tribes are small in number, together totalling not more than 200. Neighbours of the Kurasikana are the *Panare*, inhabiting the western sources of the Cuchivero, an affluent of the lower Orinoco. A tribe which is still possibly surviving to-day on the Nichare, a left-affluent of the Caura, is the *Taparito*, formerly very much feared. The *Mapoyo* once lived between the Paruaza and the Suapuré. They are reported, however, almost completely to have perished by an act of voluntary suicide in 1915. It is possible that a few are surviving. The *Kariniako* and *Kirikiripa*, of the lower Orinoco, are probably now extinct.

This completes the list of the Carib tribes of the region. They, however, are not its only inhabitants, and we will now mention the remaining groups.

Along the Sierra Pacaraima there are two very small groups which cannot be affiliated with any linguistic family and are independent of one another. The *Awaké*, reduced to a few individuals, live in a maloca (or communal house) at the sources of the Paragua and on the Uraricapara, a left-affluent of the Uraricuera in Brazilian territory. Of about the same number are the *Kaliana*. They dwell on the upper Paragua west of the Awaké.

The sources of the Orinoco on the western slopes of the Serra Parima are still held by a tribe of Indians known in Venezuela as the *Guaharibos*. Their intractable attitude and indomitable hostility have achieved for them a title to fame which commences from the year 1763. In that year the Spanish Boundary Commission alienated their sympathies. Ever since that fatal day they have dominated the sources of the river, and no explorer has yet penetrated to the actual head-waters. It is considered impossible to traverse their territory without loss of life. The Guaharibo are not a river people, but Indians of the forest only. They use neither rafts nor canoes, and in many respects appear similar to the Makú of the River Negro. " Ethnologically the Guaharibo are of interest as an extremely primitive people, who are anthropophagous, eat their food raw, and apparently possess no knowledge of fire. They have no dogs, live in circular houses on the communal plan, cultivate plantations during a part of the year, and for the remainder roam in bands over a savage wilderness bisected by the Parima Serra."* Their linguistic affiliation is unknown. It is possible that this designation covers several different tribes.

The Arawak family is represented in the region by the following tribes :—

Mixed with the Makiritare on the rivers Auari, Merevari and some of the affluents of the upper Orinoco are a few score *Guinau*. They were probably impelled into the region from the south-west by Carib pressure, and such of them as still exist are rapidly adopting the language and customs of their neighbours. Formerly the *Baré* were vitally associated with the commerce and activities of the whole Orinoco-Negro region, and they have unquestionably constituted far from a negligible factor in the composition of the civilized population of the latter river. From their original home on the Casiquiare and Pacimoni they dispersed south-west and north-west till they extended from the Maipures Rapid on the Orinoco to the lower River Negro. Only the vestiges of this far-flung population now survive. There are some families at São Marcellino on the River Negro in Brazilian territory, Solano on the Casiquiare, on a number of the smaller southern and western affluents of the

---

* Rice, A. H. " Plans for Exploration at the Headwaters of the Branco and Orinoco." *The Geographical Review*. 15 (1925), 115–122, p. 122.

famous canal, and in their old home on the Pacimoni and its source-affluent the Baria. Pathetic decimations have sadly attenuated their numbers during the lapse of 100 years. " The difficult service of rowers which the Indians practise year in and year out, sometimes to Manáos and sometimes to Ciudad Bolivar, and their retention often for half a year and longer from their homes, but especially unhealthy labour in the rubber forest during the last ten years have wrought terrible havoc among them. The drudgery for capitalism, the god of modern ' culture,' leaves them no time to till their fields. Fever and the diseases of civilization to which their weakened bodies can raise no opposition account for the remainder. . . as a tribe they have ceased to exist."*

At the sources of the Siapa and the Mauaka, a right-affluent of the upper Orinoco, are said to dwell to-day only wild Indians who have no dealings with the Indians of the Casiquiare. The region is almost entirely unexplored. Speculation designates it as the home of the *Mawaka*, and other Arawak tribes of the upper Pacimoni. The *Mandawaka*, whose dialect is related to the Arawak of the Isana, are represented by a small group at the sources of the Cauaburi, which rises close to the Baria. The *Barawana* and *Yabaana* of the Marauia and Padauiry in Brazil are both probably extinct.

The most important group of the Indians of region (3) still awaits consideration. It is the *Piaroa*. These people form a frightened and timid tribe. Misplaced confidences of the past have bred in the present generation a wholly justifiable fear of the white man, from whom they flee as speedily as before the advance of the plague. The majority speak their own dialect, which belongs to the Sáliba family, but a small number also understand Spanish. They number perhaps 2,500. They inhabit the Venezuelan affluents of the middle Orinoco from the Parguasa (Paruaza) to the Ventuari, including the Sipapo and the Cataniapo. Mixed with the *Makú*, a sub-tribe, they live in considerable numbers on the affluents of the right bank of the middle and lower Ventuari. (See also p. 45.) An independent Protestant missionary from Detroit (Michigan), has

* Koch-Grünberg, Th. " Die Völkergruppierung zwischen Rio Branco, Orinoco, Rio Negro und Yapurá." Festshrift Eduard Seler. Stuttgart, 1922. 654 pp., pp. 205–66, p. 241.

recently been successful in initiating work among them on the Parguasa.

The tribes of region (3) can be reached from two bases : (*a*) Ciudad Bolivar and (*b*) San Fernando de Atabapo. The former is the gate of the Orinoco, and the starting-point for an expedition to, say, the Piaroa. The latter, a place of 150 people, is the metropolis—mean, dirty and unhealthy though it is—of the upper region, and the capital of the territory of Amazonas. Its value as a centre of work is vitiated by its inaccessibility, its insanitary position, and the expense of supplies of food for sale. On the other hand it stands at the confluence of several rivers. Tribes of the Negro-Casiquiare region and of the upper Orinoco are also accessible from Manáos, or from any of the small centres of trade on the upper Negro. The journey, however, involves a passage through Brazilian territory.

Protestant Missions operating among the Indians of Venezuela have no continuous history. (See p. 27.) The only one working to-day is the result of an effort, initiated in 1923, to reach the Piaroas already referred to in the description of that tribe. Beyond this the nearest mission stations are in S. Fernando de Apure, where the Seventh-Day Adventist Denomination and the Assemblies of God are represented, and in Ciudad Bolivar, which is a station of the Christian Missions in Many Lands.

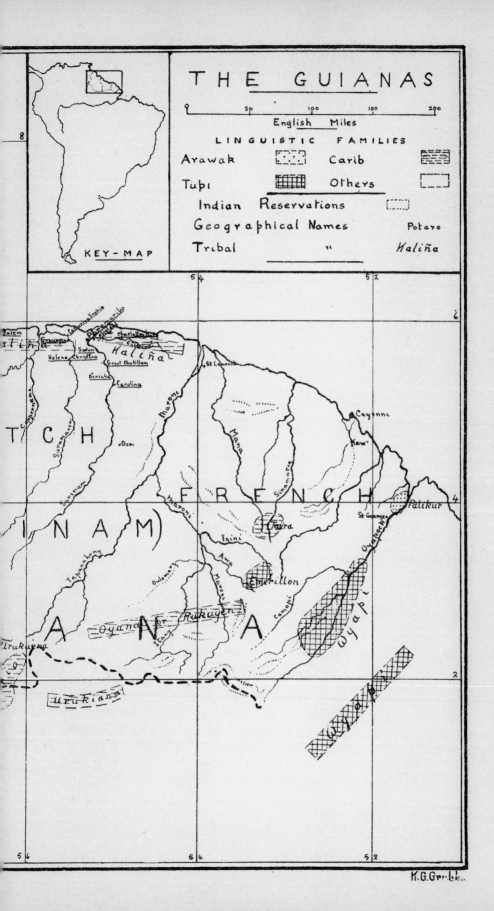

THE GUIANAS

English Miles

50   100   150   200

LINGUISTIC FAMILIES

Arawak   Carib

Tupi   Others

Indian Reservations

Geographical Names   Potaro

Tribal   „   Kaliña

KEY-MAP

K.G.Grubb.

CHAPTER IV.

THE GUIANAS

THE three Guianas, British, Dutch (Surinam) and French, constitute a section of South America which has, although a littoral region, continued to this day comparatively little exploited. British Guiana is commercially linked with the West Indies, while the remaining two are largely isolated from the coastal and river communications of Brazil. They are outside the drainage system of the Amazon river. In the watershed of the Tumuchumac and Acarai mountains is located the source-region of a number of important streams, such as the Essequibo, the Correntyne, Maroni and Oyapock, which flow into the Atlantic. The Guianas are characterized by an alternation of plains and forest land.

BRITISH GUIANA

Area. Sq. miles.	(1) Population.	(2) Indian Population.	Percentage of (1) formed by (2).	Indian Pop. per sq. mile.
90,000	301,000	12,000	4.00	.13

Capital: Georgetown (60,000). Administration: a form of limited self-administration under a Governor appointed by the Crown. Products and resources: sugar, timber, diamonds.

The population of " aborigines " returned in the census of 1921 was 9,150. The Indians of the more remote parts of the Colony are not included in this figure. They have been estimated at varying numbers, but, according to the concensus of the best information, do not amount to more than a few thousands, bringing the total up to, say, 12,000.

E

The status of the Indians in British Guiana is defined by law, and the responsibility for their protection is vested in the Commissioner of Lands and Mines. Permits must be obtained in order to employ the services of an Indian, and for labour in the remoter regions, a surety of $25 must be deposited in Georgetown for each Indian thus contracted.

Nine areas have been set apart by the Government as Reserves. These reserves are listed here briefly, with the locality, area, number and identity of Indians and religious work sustained among them.

Name.	Area sq. m.	Locality.	Tribes.	Number.	Missions.
1. Moruka ..	305	R. Moruka ..	Arawak	1,000	Anglican and R.C.
2. Wakapau	18	R. Wakapau ..		3–400	Anglican.
3. Upper Pomeroon	262	R. Pomeroon ..		250	,,
4. Iturubisi Creek ..	65	R. Iturubisi ..	Arawak	45	,,
5. Muritaro	¼	R. Demerara ..	Akawai		,,
6. Wikki Creek	95	R. Berbice ..		120	Congregational
7. Vlissingen	1½	,, ..		6	
8. Orealla ..	54	R. Correntyne	Arawak, Warau	300	Anglican.
9. Epira ..	52	,,		68	,,

Missionary work in Berbice (then under the Dutch) was commenced by the Moravian Brethren in 1738, who laboured among the Arawak Indians. To-day a number of bodies participate in Protestant effort in the colony, some of whom come into contact with the Indians. Such are the Board of Foreign Missions of the Presbyterian Church of Canada, the Wesleyan Methodist Missionary Society, the British Guiana Congregational Union, and the Christian Missions in Many Lands (Ebeny Creek and elsewhere).

The Missionary work of the Church of England was initiated in 1829 under the agency of the Church Missionary Society. This work was subsequently transferred to the S.P.G., and is now under the Bishop of British Guiana, to whom the Society makes an

annual grant. It is through the activities of the Society
for the Propagation of the Gospel that the aborigines
of the interior have reaped considerable benefits.
Their early pioneers include names greatly honoured
in the history of missions among the Indians, and
to-day they have stations in a number of localities,
as the list which follows shows.

Locality.	Station.	Tribe.
North-West District	St. Hilda's, Warapoko Creek (R. Waini)	Arawak, Warau
,,	St. Hubert's, Arahaka, R. Barama ..	
,,	St. Bede's, R. Barama	Karib.
Pomeroon District	St. James, Waramuri	
,,	St. Matthias, Cabacaburi	
,,	St. Lucian, Wakapoa (R. Pomeroon)	
Essequibo River	St. Denys, Tapacooma (R. Essequibo)	
,, ..	Dufferyn Mission and Iturubisi ..	Arawak.
	Creek Reservation	
,, ..	Bartika Grove	Akawai, Arawak.
Rupununi River	Eupukari	Makushi, Partamona, Wapisiana.
Demerara ..	Santa, Camuni Creek (R. Demerara)..	Arawak.
,, ..	St. Hugh, Muritaro, (R. Demerara) ..	Akawai.
,, ..	St. Saviour, Mallali (R. Demerara) ..	,,
,, ..	St. Cuthbert, Mahaica Creek	Arawak.
Berbice River ..	St. Peter, Sandhills	Arawak.
Correntyne River	Orealla	Arawak, Warau

The activities of the Roman Catholic Church are
invested in the English Jesuits, whose work amongst
the Indians dates from 1855. More recently a Mission
has been opened in the Rupununi district, with its
principal station entitled St. Ignatius, on the Takutu.

We will now describe the various tribes in order :

The *Akawai* are found west and north-west of the Essequibo,
on the Mazaruni, Cuyuni and Pomeroon, and at the sources
of the Waini, Barama and Barima. East of the Essequibo,
on the upper Demerara and Berbice, they are known as Waika.
They wander over extensive tracts of country and share the
Carib propensity for trading. The true " *Karib*," who include
remnants of other tribes, are found on the upper Barima,
Barama and Cuyuni. Something of the respect which their
bellicosity formerly commanded is retained towards them

among other tribes to-day. The *Arekuna*, who have been referred to under Venezuela (see p. 60), are established to the north of Mt. Roraima and also south-west of this famous mountain as far as the Island of Maracá in Brazil. They are savannah dwellers, but inhabit also the edge of the forest. A few of their huts are encountered on the left-affluents of the Uraricuera. Within this delimitation we have included the so-called Taulipang, who appear to be merely a section of the Arekuna, the two groups totalling less than 3,000. The Arekuna, who originally migrated from the water-shed between the Essequibo and the Jauapery, have not exhibited the characteristics of a powerful and cohesive people. The *Partamona* occupy the country between the Potaro and the Ireng. They are identical with the so-called Ingariko, this term being a designation employed by the Makushi. The *Seregong*, related to the Partamona, constitute a small group apparently at the sources of the Cotingo.

The *Makushi* are the predominant Carib tribe of the interior. In addition to the handsomeness of their physical appearance, they can claim a certain attractiveness of disposition and refinement of manner. While maintaining a pacific attitude towards strangers and other tribes, they have preserved many of their customs to this day intact. Like so many Indians, they have not escaped the ravages of epidemics of disease. Missionary work under the Bishop of British Guiana was initiated by a pioneer journey in 1907, and has been attended with gratifying results. (See also p. 28.) The Makushi live on the Ireng or Mahú, the Takutu and Rupununi, and on both sides of the boundary between Brazil and British Guiana. For preference, however, they select the Canucu and Pacaraima mountains, and extend from these to the Cotingo. They are encountered, mixed with the Wapisiana, on the eastern point of the Island of Maracá and on the Surumú and Uraricuera. A number of separate groups are recognized among them. The Wai-wai, who are doubtless identical with the Wyawé (see p. 107), live in very reduced numbers on the Kamacoko, an eastern branch of the Essequibo. All the tribes hitherto mentioned belong to the Carib family, in which also may be classed the Akuria and the Chakoi, whose existence is problematical. They have, however, been reported in very small numbers between the upper Demerara and Berbice rivers, and on the River Tuira, localities in which they are said to be living in a very primitive state.

The Indian occupation of British Guiana is not limited to these, and it is necessary to mention the following groups :—

The *Wapisiana* are neighbours of the Makushi. They are encountered at the sources of the Takutu and Rupununi, where they are dwellers of the savannah or plain. They are also met between the Takutu and the River Branco in Brazilian territory, on the lower Uraricuera (right bank), on the lower Cotingo west to the mountains south of the Sutumu and on the Parimé-Marua to the lower Majary. They have completely absorbed their neighbours the Atorai, a small tribe. The Wapisiana are scattered over a comprehensive area, but they do not, probably, number more than 3,000. They are a peaceful people who engage in trade, some of whom speak, in addition to their own dialect, Portuguese or English, and sometimes Makushi. The *Taruma* are encountered on the right bank of the upper Essequibo above the Cuduwini. The *Mapidian*, who, strictly speaking, dwell in Brazil, are mentioned here for the sake of convenience. They live between the upper Mapu-erwau and the Apiniwau, in the source-region of the Trombetas. These two tribes do not total more than 200.

In addition to these tribes of the Arawak family we close the list for British Guiana with a reference to the *Warau*. These Indians, who have been discussed under Venezuela (see p. 59), occupy, in British Guiana, the north-west coast region adjacent to the boundary with the latter republic. They must be regarded as linguistically independent. Some of them are Christians.

Missionary work among the Indians of British Guiana has already been referred to. The tribes are all accessible from Georgetown, the capital, by travelling on the rivers of the country. Frequently rapids prove a troublesome but by no means insuperable barrier to communication. The journey from George-town to the furthest station of the S.P.G. situated on the Rupununi occupies between three and four weeks.

DUTCH GUIANA (SURINAM)

Areas. Sq. miles.	(1) Population.	(2) Indian Population.	Percentage of (1) formed by (2).	Indian Pop. per sq. mile.
46,000	134,000	3,500	2.61	.08

Capital : Paramaribo (45,000). Administration : the Colony is administered by a Governor assisted by a Council appointed by the Home Government. Resources and products : sugar, bauxite.

Population. The official report for the Colony returns the Indian population at 2,645. The census did not, however, make any attempt to cover the few remaining representatives of the interior tribes, and it is to allow for these that we have raised the total to 3,500.

Missionary work in Surinam is almost entirely under the control of the Missions Direktion der Brüdergemeine (Moravian Brethren), whose baptized and communicant membership is 26,000. The Moravian Brethren commenced work in 1738, and the Arawak Indians rapidly came under their influence. To-day, with the decline of the Indian population, this branch of the work has become of decreasing importance.

Roman Catholics are represented by the Dutch Redemptorists, whose Indian activities have extended to the Kaliña tribe.

The remnants of the *Kaliña*, Galibi or Karaib are found at various points near the coast between the Maroni and the Correntyne. This tribe originally was dispersed over an immense area, being discovered by the first white invaders in considerable numbers in the lesser Antilles. The *Trio* dwell in reduced numbers at the sources of the Paloumeu and the Correntyne and also on the Brazilian side of the divide. The *Kumayena* and *Urukuena* are reported to be very small groups on the Karope, an eastern affluent of the Cutari or upper Correntyne. The most celebrated Indians of the interior are the *Oyana*, known in French Guiana as the Rukuyen, and in Brazil as the Urukiana. Without doubt, the Urukuena are to be identified also with these. In Surinam they are found on the Paloumeu and upper Tapanahoni, and in French Guiana on the upper Itany and affluents. In Brazil they are known on the upper Jary and Parú, where they have incorporated the Upurui. It is probable that to-day they do not number more than a few hundreds. The Rukuyen had, in times past, a reputation for savagery.

All these tribes are of Carib family. The Indians of the interior have never been visited by a missionary. They are accessible by ascending the rivers Correntyne, Maroni, etc., which rise in the divide between the Guianas and Brazil.

FRENCH GUIANA

Area. Sq. miles.	(1) Population.	(2) Indian Population.	Percentage of (1) formed by (2).	Indian Pop. per sq. mile.
24,000	55,000	1,400*	2.55	.06

Capital : Cayenne (10,000). Administration : the Governor is assisted by a small council. The colony sends a deputy to the legislative assembly in Paris. Resources and products : gold.

The colony has had a sinister and discouraging history. It is well called the " white man's grave " of South America. There has never been any attempt to initiate Protestant Missions, either among the Indians or the white population. The capital, Cayenne, is a town of moderate size, and is accessible by sea from Georgetown (435 miles) or Paramaribo, the capital of Surinam (225 miles). St. George on the Oyapock has a monthly steamer communication with Pará in Brazil.

Romanist missions are not represented to-day among the Indians. Missionary work was initiated by the arrival of two Dominicans in 1560, who were immediately murdered by the Indians, and in 1643 two Capuchins similarly suffered a violent death. The pacification of the Kaliña was undertaken by the Jesuits in 1639.

As usual, we confine our description to the Indian tribes of whom there survive the following :—

The *Taira* are found at the sources of the Mana and the Sinamarie.

The *Rukuyen* have been referred to under Dutch Guiana (see p. 70). Both these tribes are Carib.

The *Emerillon* have deserted the Approuague, where they formerly lived, and are now found, in reduced numbers, on the Awa and on the Inini, a right-affluent of the Maroni.

---

* A census of the colony was taken in 1921, and the figure represents the best estimate available.

The *Wyapí*, or Oyampí, who live largely in Brazil, are reported on both banks of the upper Oyapock. Both the Emerillon and the Wyapí are Tupi tribes.

The *Palikur*. A section of this tribe has been established since 1900 on the left bank of the estuary of the Oyapock on the creek Marouane. Many are now deculturized and influenced by creole civilization. These Indians, belonging to the Arawak family, number about 200.

This completes the list of such tribes as are still surviving in French Guiana. Coudreau, in 1888, stated that there were twenty tribes within the colony, totalling 20,000 souls.*

---

* Coudreau, H. "La Haute Guyane." *Revue de Géographie.* Paris. 23 (1888), 247–70, p. 264.

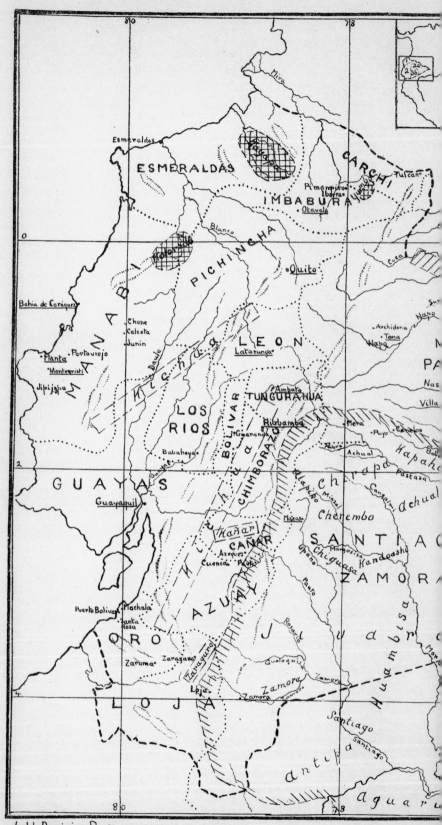

KEY-MAP
Figures in-
dicate divi-
sions in text.

E C U A D O R

0   50   100   150
English   Miles

LINGUISTIC   FAMILIES

Chibcha   Jivaro

Zaparo   Others

Geographical Names   Pastaza
Tribal   "   Cherembo

Aguarico

Napo

Putumayo

Yasuni

Nashino

Tambor-Yacu

Napo

Curaray

N A P O -

Yano-Yacu   Orejone

Andoas

Tigre

P A S T A Z A

Pastaza

Huasaga

Corrientes

Pucacuro

Mazan

urato

Iquitos

L. Rimachiuma

Nanay

Chambira

Nacuray   Orito-Yacu

Marañon

K. G. Grubb

CHAPTER V.

ECUADOR

Region.	Area. Sq. miles.	(1) Population.	(2) Indian Pop.	Percentage of (1) formed by (2).	Indian Pop. per sq. mile.
Andean Section ..	65,000	2,000,000	600,000	30.00	9.23
Lowland ,, ..	55,000	80,000	25,000	31.25	.45

Capital : Quito (100,000). Government : Republican. The President is elected for four years. Ecuador has had eleven constitutions since 1830. Resources and products : Cacao, sugar, bananas, oil. Panama hats form a prominent manufacture.

IN discussing the Indians we shall observe three divisions :

(1) The Kolorado and Kayapa. 2,500 Indians.
(2) The Kichua Indians of the Sierras. 600,000 Indians.
(3) The Oriente. 25,000 Indians.

The first two of these divisions occupy the mountains, the inter-Andine valley, and the coastal plain, but the last represents the forest region of the upper Amazon basin.

(1) *The Kolorado and the Kayapa.* 2,500 Indians.

These two tribes constitute the southern extension of the Chibcha linguistic family into Ecuador. They are undoubtedly relations of the Kwaiker and Telembi, described on p. 40, and are certainly connections of one another.

The *Kolorado* are found in the department of Manabi. They occupy the sources of some of the left-affluents of the River Blanco, affluent of the Esmeraldas, and are met near the village of Santo Domingo, 36 leagues from Quito. Two hundred or more are scattered in small groups in the forest two to four leagues from the village. A village of 100 is established in the same vicinity near San Miguel. They total between 300 and 400, all retaining their own Chibcha language, but some in addition exhibiting an acquaintance with Spanish. They serve no common chief, and live in comparative social seclusion, one family in a house.

The *Kayapa* enjoy a position of greater importance. They are located in the northern province of Esmeraldas along the course of the River Cayapas and its affluents.   Their territory is easily attained from seaward, and some of the Indians themselves indulge in annual visits to the ocean. The Kayapas number between 1,500 and 2,000. Their dialect, though of the same family, is almost unintelligible to the Kolorados, with whom they have little contact, and their customs are distinct. Some of the men have with difficulty learned Spanish, but social etiquette forbids its acquisition by the women. They do no metal work, though it is of interest to note that platinum was early discovered in the province of Esmeraldas. Their standard of ethics is high, but their aboriginal ceremonies have been displaced by the ceremonial of Rome. They are visited once a year by the priest. No Protestant work has been attempted among them. The Jesuits were constituted in 1922 as a " mission to the heathen " in the province of Manabi.

(2) *The Kichua Indians of the Sierras.* 600,000 Indians.

The discussion of the distribution and present condition of these Indians will not be undertaken here for two reasons. Firstly, the primary object of this survey is to deal with the lowland tribes, and secondly, they are fully considered in the report by Dinwiddie on the republic.* I limit myself here to advancing a few conclusions of a historico-linguistic character. Kichua is spoken to-day in all the inter-andine valley of Ecuador. Its wide distribution is due to two causes : (i.) The expansion of the Inca empire as far as the

---

* A missionary survey of Ecuador was made by H. B. Dinwiddie, of the Pioneer Mission Agency, in 1923, and reference should be made to the report of his findings. Dinwiddie, H. B. " Ecuador : A Missionary Survey." New York, 1924. 40 pp.

present boundaries of Colombia and Ecuador. (ii.) Its use by the early Spanish conquerors and missionaries. The domination established under (i.) was sufficient to enforce authoritatively the use of Kichua as a language of civilization. It failed, however, to abolish such independent groups as the Puruhá and the Esmeralda. The names of some of these have continued to this day, and their identity is recognized in the occurrence of different types as the Kañari and the so-called Zaraguro. At the time of the conquest the rank and file of these nations spoke their own dialects, but under the influence of (ii.) they speedily adopted the language of the more powerful race (Kichua). The dialect of Kichua employed in Ecuador is known as the Kiteño. These Indians constitute the bulk of the pure-blooded Indian population of Ecuador, which, according to Dinwiddie* (p. 74), is not less than 600,000. The stations of Missions working in this area are shown in the map of Ecuador.

(3) *The Oriente.* 25,000 Indians.

Few attempts have been made to analyse this region hitherto in any published missionary survey, and I shall therefore mention the tribes in some detail. By a decree of November 25th, 1920, the Oriente was divided into two provinces : (*a*) Napo-Pastaza, and (*b*) Santiago-Zamora, with their capitals at Tena and Zamora respectively. Both these regions include a number of Kichua-speaking Indians along the cordillera. These are discussed concisely in Dinwiddie's admirable sketch.

The Indians of province (*a*) belong principally to the *Zaparo.* They live in the plantations of the civilized people on the River Napo, where they speak Kichua. To the north of the Napo, near the River Suna, there is a settlement of some 500 Indians. Sixty-two tribes and sub-tribes of the Zaparos have been recorded, a number reduced by careful revision to twenty-nine, but most of them have become extinct, and the remainder are rapidly losing distinctive identity. Though the

---

* Dinwiddie, H. B. Op. cit.

Zaparos were inferior as a nation to the Jivaro, they engaged in agriculture and constructed settled abodes. Among tribes of this family that persist are the *Yasuni* on the river of that name ; the *Andoa* and *Pinche* in two miserable villages not far below the confluence of the Bobonaza and the Pastaza ; and the *Zaparo*, properly so-called, mingled, as already mentioned, with the civilized population of the Napo and the Curaray.

Between these latter two rivers there lives a savage tribe termed the *Auka*, which in Kichua means " barbarian." These Indians are, as their vocabulary shows, of Zaparo family, and are mixed with some wild Abijira (Avishiri) and Kuraraye of Tukano family. They number about 2,000, and include such Zaparo sub-tribes as the Nushino and Supinu, etc., whose names are recorded in the toponymy of the region. A few are encountered in captivity on the River Napo.

In addition there are 200 *Orejone* Indians of the Witoto family on the Yano-yacu, a right-affluent of the Curaray, near its confluence with the Napo.

The Indians of province (*a*) may total 5,000–10,000, and apart from the Aukas, who speak Zaparo, generally communicate in Kichua.

(*b*) The Province of Santiago-Zamora. From the earliest times this has been the hereditary property of the *Jivaro* Indians.

This group, including numerous tribes and sub-tribes, has always enjoyed a certain notoriety. Their peculiar customs and accessibility have constantly invited exploration and enquiry, but their often savage treatment of strangers has led to the maintenance of their independence. Their history has been eventful. In 1599, for example, the governor of Macas, on the accession of Philip III., tried to raise tribute from them. The Jivaros united to regain their freedom by the fortunes of a single raid. To the number of 20,000 they assaulted the town of Logroño by night, massacring the inhabitants and levelling the houses to the ground. The governor was compelled to drain a cup of the molten gold which in his greed

he had desired so much to obtain. Led by their chief
Quiruba they then surprised Mendoza, where the
18,000 inhabitants fell as victims to this unexpected
attack. Three avenging expeditions failed miserably
of their object.

To-day the Jivaro live in communal houses divided
into numerous sub-tribes of some 100–200 souls in each.
From time to time these groups unite in war against
each other, due partly to the necessities of polygamy,
but mostly owing to the incapability of a Jivaro con-
ceiving death to be a natural process. He believes it to
have been wrought by the incantation of the enemy,
for which revenge must be consequently meted out.

The habit of head-hunting has made these people
notorious. The skull is removed from the fleshy parts
and the latter, by moulding over stones of successively
decreasing size, is reduced to a repulsive miniature
which preserves with remarkable exactness the features
of the original. Head-hunting is not peculiar to the
Jivaro ; it was also a practice of the Mundurukú.
Scalping was practised formerly both in the Chaco
and in Guiana.

The Jivaro language has been attested by a
variety of documents, some of considerable value.
" In the language of the Jíbaros is reflected the ener-
getic and vehement character of these Indians, and
many sounds, for this reason, have a much harder
and rougher pronunciation than in European languages.
Besides, we must notice that the Jíbaro does not
express his thoughts and feelings only with words,
but also with mimic and every class of signs, with
movements of the hands and feet, of the head and the
whole body, on certain occasions also with the arms,
the lance and the shield. It is necessary to take into
account these accessory means of expression to have a
perfect idea of the language of these Indians."* The

* Karsten, Rafael. " La Lengua de los Indios Jíbaros (Shuãra)
del Oriente del Ecuador. Gramatica, vocabulario y muestras de la
prosa y poesia. Översikt av Finska Vetenskaps-Societetens Forhand-
lingar." Helsingfors. Vol. LXIV. 1921–22. Avd. B. No. 2. pp. 1–65,
p. 6.

family has not yet been united with any other, though it seems to include a number of Arawak elements. There are not a few dialectical differences between the different tribes. It has no connection with that of the now extinct Jevero of an adjacent locality.

Geographically they occupy a vaguely triangular territory bounded on the south by the Marañon (including the Aguaruna on the right bank), on the west by the Andes, and on the north-east and east by the Pastaza. This includes a region in the north of Peru, which is included in this discussion for the sake of convenience. The Jivaro are most conveniently listed by grouping them round three affluents of the Marañon, which traverse their territory : (i.) The Pastaza ; (ii.) The Morona ; (iii.) The Santiago. But it should be remembered that the various sub-tribes are so constantly engaged in disturbances of one kind or another that any attempt to list them geographically becomes of problematical value.

(i.) The Pastaza.

The *Huamboyas* live between the sources of the Palora and the Llusino, and in the mountains north of the volcano Sangay. The *Palora* occupy the river of that name. The *Achuale*, a much more important group, claim the right bank of the Pastaza from the River Achual to the confluence of the Bobonaza. It was they who annihilated the Andoas. Between the Bobonaza and Pastaza and their affluents of this section live the *Pindu, Kopatasa* and *Kapahuari*. The *Murato* and *Machine* are established some distance to the south of the Achuale between the Pastaza and the Morona, on the rivers which flow into the lake Rimachiuma and on the Huito Yaco, Chimara and Manchari, right-affluents of the Pastaza. These tribes together number some 400, and with the Achuale they form the most important groups on the river.

(ii.) The Morona.

In this region we include the more prominent group of the *Chirapa* between the Palora and Miazal. To the south of them descending the river we encounter a number of small groups on affluents which frequently bear their names : the *Chihuando, Cherembo*, to the east of Macas ; the *Mangosisa, Kangaime, Kandoashi*, together with three sub-tribes of the Murato and Machine. But the principal tribe and one of the most important of the Jivaro nation is the *Huambisa*, who exceed, perhaps, 1,000 souls, and occupy the forest between the lower Morona and Santiago.

(iii.) The Santiago.

Briefly enumerated, the Indians of this basin are :

On the left bank of the Upano : the *Chiguasa* and two other sections.

On the right bank of the Upano : the *Alapiko* and four neighbouring sections.

About 40–50 Catholicized Alapiko Indians are found on the River Palora. The sub-tribes on the Zamora, Yacumbi, Paute and Gualaquiza bear the names of these rivers and range in number from 50 to 400. These are also found : On the River Bomboiza, *Naranza* ; Rivers Cuchipamba and Cuye, *Jivaros* of Tuledu, *Indanza, Yunganza* ; River Santiago, the so-called *Santiago*, who include the *Iransa, Patokuma*, etc. The most prominent of all these sub-divisions is undoubtedly the *Antipa*, who dwell to the west of the lower Santiago.

South of the Marañon, in Peruvian territory, is found a further important tribe, the *Aguaruna*.

Many other groups are known, but the Indians are most conveniently summed up as Pastazas, Moronas or Santiagos. Their total number is between 15,000 and 20,000. Some indeed consider it much less, while others give as much as 50,000, allotting to the whole Oriente an Indian population of not less than 200,000.

Dinwiddie selects Mera as pre-eminently the strategic centre for region (3). In his report will be found a mass of information on communications and present missionary work. The aim of the present survey is to provide information which, owing to the difficulty of obtaining it, is not available elsewhere. The Franciscans are established at Zamora and the Dominicans at Canelos and Macas, while the apostolic vicariat of Mendez and Gualaquiza has been allotted to the Salesians. (See also p. 136.) Protestant Missionary effort is represented by the Gospel Missionary Union at Sukula, near Macas, while at the latter place, and at Tena (which is frequently visited by Indians known as Archidonians), the Christian and Missionary Alliance are represented. (See also p. 85 and maps.)

CHAPTER VI.

PERU

Region.	Area. Sq. miles.	(1) Popu- lation.	(2) Indian Pop.	Percentage of (1) formed by (2).	Indian Pop. per sq. mile.
Andean Section ..	284,000	5,000,000	3,400,000	68.00	11.97
Lowland ,, ..	250,000	200,000	71,000	35.50	.28

Capital : Lima (220,000). Government : Republican. Authority is invested in a Senate of thirty-five members and a House of Representatives of 110. The President is elected for five years. In 1922 an organization was created, under the Presidency of the Archbishop of Lima, entitled the " Patronato de la raza indigena." By making representations to the government the declared aim was to improve the condition of the Indians by protective legislation.

" Recently the ' Regional Federation of Indians ' has been organized, purporting to represent 4,000,000 Indians, but it is not well organized, and its principal work is that of sending communications to the daily papers about the abuses committed constantly against the Indians by political and ecclesiastical authorities, and by a certain type of merchants, landowners and miners."*

Resources and products : Sugar, cotton, fruit, wool, copper, silver, petroleum. British capital invested in Peru : £27,000,000.

FOR a detailed consideration of the Indians of Peru we prefer three divisions :

(1) The Kichua-speaking Indians of the Cordilleras. 3,400,000 Indians.

(2) The basins of the Ucayali and the Huallaga. 31,000 Indians.

(3) The Kampa Indians and sub-tribes. 30,000– 40,000 Indians.

---

* " Christian Work in South America." Vol. I., p. 428.

(1) *The Kichua-speaking Indians* of the Cordilleras.*
3,400,000 Indians.

The most recent official estimates of the Indian
population of Peru return 3,459,600 for a total, and of
these some 3,400,000 are required for the civilized
Kichua Indians of the highlands. " The Kichua or
Runasimi is the only language of South America
which had played in the pre-Colombian epoch the
part of a language of civilization ; propagated by the
conquering Incas it spread little by little throughout
nearly the whole of their vast empire, of which it became
the official language, and where it played a rôle of a
language of liaison."† It is generally agreed that the
Indians of North Peru are acquainted with Spanish
to a much greater degree than those in the south.
Historically, as in Ecuador, Kichua displaced a number
of other different tribal languages, and under the
influence of the early missionaries it penetrated to the
sources of the north-western affluents of the Amazon,
to the Ucayali, to the upper Amazon itself, and to the
basin of the Beni.

The principal dialects, according to Rivet, are the Lamano
or Lamista, the Chinchasuyu or Chinchaya with the sub-
dialects of Huari in the departments of Ancachs, of Huanuco,
and of Cajamarca ; the dialect of the province of Huancayo
in the department of Junin ; of Ayacucho ; and the Kuskeño
spoken in the neighbourhood of Cuzco. The density of the
Indian population is greater in the south than in the north.

In addition to Kichua, *Aymara* is spoken in certain
parts of southern Peru. The Lupaka on the south-west
shore of Lake Titicaca in the department of Puno
employ it, the domain of their language here extending
as far north as Puno. The Kolagua live to the north-
west of Arequipa on the River Colca, and at the
sources of the Vitor, while the Kauki, an Aymara dialect,
is still used in the department of Lima in the villages
of Tupe, Huaquis, Laraas, and elsewhere.

---

* For a similar reason to that assigned in the case of Ecuador (see
p. 74), we make no attempt to deal extensively with this section.

† Rivet, P. In " Les Langues du Monde." Op. cit. p. 666.

F

Six American and three British societies are working in Peru.   The Evangelical Union of South America have a flourishing agricultural mission at Urco.   The Christian and Missionary Alliance are established at Huancayo, while the Seventh-Day Adventist Denomination have seventy schools for Indians in the neighbourhood of Puno and Lake Titicaca.

(2) *The basins of the Ucayali and the Huallaga.*   31,000 Indians.

We shall consider the tribes of this region working from the interior to the coast, dealing with (*a*) the area to the north of the Marañon, and (*b*) the area south of the main river.

(*a*) The *Witoto* Indians occupy the disputed area between Colombia and Peru.   They have been already referred to in dealing with the former republic (see p. 54).   Their natural home has always been between the Caquetá and the Içá and on the rivers Carapaná and Igará-paraná.   During the years 1903–10 they were completely disorganized and subjected to many cruelties arising from the exploration of the region for wild rubber.   To-day nearly all in Peruvian territory are domesticated, and they form the bulk of the 10,000 Indians employed in the territory of the Peruvian Amazon Company who hold a title to 14,200,000 acres of land in the Putumayo region. Nearly all understand some Spanish.   The Witoto otherwise form a distinct linguistic family.   A list of their sub-tribes embraces 151 names.

The *Miranya* or Boro, formerly estimated at 15,000, were decimated through the oppression which completely destroyed the tribal life of this region.   The survivors are now dispersed among the various civilized settlements of the adjacent rivers.   They all speak Spanish to-day.   Their original tongue must be regarded as independent.   A small group may be found in Brazilian territory, on the south bank of the Solimões, a little west of Teffé.   The *Yagua, Peba*, and *Yameo* live on the small affluents of the left bank of the Marañon between Long. 69° 30′ and 75°.   Far the greater part are now civilized and engaged in rubber activities.   The *Tikuna* are represented in Peruvian territory north of the Amazon by small remnants between the Ambiyacu and the Atacuary. They speak a corrupt Arawak dialect.

The Indians who live on Peruvian soil contiguous to the frontier of Ecuador, have been included in the discussion of the Jivaro and Zaparo families of Ecuador.

(b) The area south of the main river.

This area is characterized by the important linguistic family of the Pano. The tribes of this family are limited geographically to this section in Peru and the adjacent territory in Brazil as far as the Madeira. In other words, their natural habitat is confined to the southern and western affluents of the Amazon and the territory within a comparatively short distance of the foothills of the Andes. The primitive customs of many of the Pano tribes have been profoundly modified through the nature of their external contacts. Traces of Inca cosmogony, on the one hand, infiltrated into the valley of the Ucayali and as far east as the upper Jurua. On the other hand, the earlier chroniclers remind us that the Pano subsequently came under the regime of the missions which were first established among them in 1686. This ecclesiastical domination continued till 1768, when the Indians, provoked by diseases introduced from abroad and angered by the contemplation of their wretched condition, rebelled and demanded their freedom. Of the 150 stations which had been established in the 18th century, in 1875 only nine survived. More recently there has been a revival of Romanist effort on the Ucayali.

The *Mayoruna* or Mayo (mayo=river, runa=man, Kichua) occupy the region between the Javary, the Solimões and the Ucayali, being found on the banks of the Tapiche and upper River Blanco, right-affluents of the Ucayali, on the Javary-chico and Galvez, left-affluents of the Javary, on the Curuça and Itecoahy, right-affluents in Brazilian territory, and on some of the right-affluents of the Marañon in this region. Some are domesticated, but a number are still wild. As very small sub-tribes we mention the Marubo and the Pisabu on the River Galvez. The *Kapanawa* occupy the River Pardo, a left-affluent of the Curuça and the headwaters of the streams between the Alacran, a right-affluent of the Ucayali and the Javary. They are hostile. A few *Sensi* are found on the River Chanaya, a right-affluent of the Ucayali. A few dozen *Katukina* are still said to be scattered on the Javary. The *Remo*, now greatly reduced in numbers, inhabit the upper Javary and its right- and left-affluents to Bathan, Galvez, Blanco and the right-affluents of the Ucayali to the Utuquinea. They continue hostile, and with the Brazilian section do not exceed 800 to-day. The Mananagua are a sub-tribe of these Indians.

The *Amahuaka* are the most important of these tribes east of the Ucayali. They total perhaps 3,000 souls with their sub-tribes, some of whose names are known to us. They have increasingly been captured by a process of domestication and labour under the patronage of the rubber gatherers. Some maintain their independence, but are hostile. Such are those on the Vacapista, a source-affluent of the Juruá and the Espino in Brazilian territory, a sub-tribe, together with some on the Chesea, a right-affluent of the Ucayali. Those on the Amoenya are friendly but independent. Geographically the Amahuaka in Peruvian territory are divided into (*a*) a group between the Curumahá and the Purus; (*b*) the main body on the divide between the Juruá, Purus, Tacuatimanu and the Ucayali, and on the right-affluents of the latter river from the Tamaya to the Mishagua.

The tribes hitherto mentioned are those which occupy the right bank of the Ucayali.

The *Shipibo*, *Shetebo* and *Konibo* are often grouped together under the name of Chama. These tribes are largely mingled and live to-day in a state of domestication along both banks of the Ucayali and the small lakes near the river. They total perhaps 3,000. The Shetebo are principally encountered between Orellana and Contamana, the Shipibo between the latter place and Iparia, and the Konibo between Iparia and Sheloga. Nearly all can converse in Spanish. They may be found concentrated at certain spots on the Ucayali with a priest working among them. The Sinabu are a sub-tribe of the Shipibo.

The *Kashibo* occupy the affluents of the left bank of the Ucayali from the Pisqui to the Pachitea. They are the most savage of the Pano tribes of the Ucayali, and are cannibals. Occasionally one is encountered in captivity on the Ucayali. They are closely related to the Kashinawa of the Tarauacá, the addition " nawa " in Pano signifying " man," while the suffix " bo " indicates the plural. It is customary to estimate the Kashibo at 3,000, possibly a correct estimate.

The Pano tribes thus sketched total between 10,000 and 12,000. The remaining tribes of this locality will be mentioned under region (3). I conclude the present list by referring to some groups of different origin.

The *Kokama* and *Kokamilla* are found along the lower Huallaga and Ucayali as far as Tierra Blanca and between these two rivers. They are tri-lingual, speaking their own dialect, which is a pure Tupi, Kichua and Spanish. Two Romanist missions are among them. Incorporated into the civilized population of the Marañon and Solimões is another Tupi tribe, the *Omagua*. The *Cholona* and *Hibito* live on the left bank of the Huallaga and its affluents between the Monzon and Pachiza. They constitute an independent linguistic family, but to-day speak Kichua.

These tribes perhaps total 4,000, giving section 2 (*b*) a total of some 16,000, while to (*a*) may be allotted 15,000, being 31,000 Indians for the whole region.

The Christian and Missionary Alliance have investigated the region, and some of the above information is drawn from their report, of which an outline was published in the " Atlas showing Mission Fields of the Christian and Missionary Alliance."* Iquitos has been occupied by the Inland South America Missionary Union during 1926. Representatives of the Seventh-Day Adventist Denomination have visited the same place, with a view to occupying the valley of the Ucayali with a base at Pucalpa. The Board of Foreign Missions of the Church of the Nazarene is represented by two missionaries among the Aguaruna (see p. 79), where their efforts have met with a gratifying response.

There has been a revival of Roman Catholic interest in the region, as mentioned on p. 83, but little has been accomplished. Priests are stationed at Iquitos, at Yurimaguas, Requena on the Ucayali, Yarina-cocha and other points.

Although Lima furnishes a convenient base for certain parts of the region, facilities for the transport of heavy supplies are better sought in Iquitos, which

* Revised Edition. New York, 1924.

is in frequent steamer communication with Europe and America. The journey between Lima and Iquitos at present takes over three weeks, but will soon be shortened by an air route. For the Indians of the Marañon west of Iquitos, Yurimaguas is the most suitable base. Further information on communications can be found in the Atlas already referred to.

(3) *The Kampa Indians and sub-tribes.*   30,000–40,000 Indians.

We have chosen to consider these Indians separately owing to their importance as a unit.

The *Kampa* (or Anti) are an Arawak tribe. They are to-day one of the most, if not the most important nation, in the whole of the area covered in this survey. Their sub-tribes include the Kamatika, Kimbiri, Pangoa, Katongo, Kimiairi, Macheyenga (Mesheringa), Pukapakuri, Unini, Ungonino, etc., of which by far the most prominent is the Macheyenga. They total, perhaps, 35,000, of whom the Macheyenga account for 10,000–15,000.* They live (*a*) on the Urubamba and tributaries ; (*b*) on the Tambo and tributaries ; (*c*) in a triangular territory bounded by the rivers Perené, Pachitea-Pichis, and upper Ucayali.

(*a*) On the Urubamba and tributaries.

As well as the Kampa proper, the Pukapakuri and the Macheyenga are encountered here. The former extend to the River Manu, an affluent of the upper Madre de Dios of the system of the Madeira. They are found on the banks of the Manu and its right-affluents west of the Pilcopata over to the Urubamba, where they inhabit this river and its right-affluents from the Camisea to the Yanatile, including the Paucartambo or Yavero. The Macheyenga have shown an increasing tendency to withdraw from the basin of the Madre de Dios.

(*b*) On the Tambo and its tributaries.

Here the Macheyenga, the Kampa, the Katongo, etc., are established on the Ene, Perené, Apurimac, Pangoa, Mantaro and right-affluents of the Ene-Apurimac.

---

* This number agrees with the usually accepted estimates, but seems to me excessive.

(*c*) The triangular territory bounded by the rivers Perené, Pachitea-Pichis, and upper Ucayali.

This is characterized by a plateau known as the Gran Pajonal, which, while maintaining an average of 4,000 feet, rises at the northern apex to 10,500 feet. Its slopes are densely forested, but the more elevated ground provides open land suitable for pasture. The bulk of the Kampa nation is located in this territory, including the Kampa proper, the Unini, Kamatika, etc. They dwell on the San Carlos range, and at the headwaters of the Unini and affluents of the Pachitea from the Nazareteque to the Apurukiali. It is in this region that they exhibit the greatest hostility.

Taken as a whole, the Kampa are unfriendly in their own homes, but friendly on their visits to the whites. They are not reluctant to work if well treated, and a number are already in the employment of the civilized people. They are, however, divided into hostile factions among themselves. The Macheyenga have exhibited a more amicable disposition than the Kampa proper, while among the more embittered must be classed those of the Tambo and Unini.

The tribal organization of the Kampa is not strong. The Macheyenga, for example, have no chief and no tribal assemblies. Each village is composed of two or three families living together. They are not conspicuous for their handicraft, and in times past, at least, have always obtained their finer pottery from the Konibo by exchange. Garments are woven and worn by the Macheyenga. Monogamy is common, but a man may have as many wives as he can support. Their superstitions are but vaguely defined. "They make no offerings or prayers, and have no ceremonies, chiefs, or fetishes. There is no communion between themselves and any spirit."*

The Kampa, as already mentioned, are an Arawak tribe, and their dialect is well attested by numerous documents. There are many dialectical differences, even among the Macheyenga themselves and between other branches.

* Farabee, William Curtis. "Indian Tribes of Eastern Peru." Papers of the Peabody Museum of American Archaeology and Ethnology, Harvard University. Vol. X., 1922. 194 pp., p. 15.

The remaining tribes of this region, though of vastly less importance, must now be mentioned : the *Piro* or Chontakiro live between the sources of the Purus and Urubamba and on the right bank of the latter river. Popularly held to be a large tribe, successive reductions have only left them about 1,000 individuals, with a few remnants on the River Aracá, a right-affluent of the Purus. The *Kushitineri* are found on the Curimahá. A part of the upper course of the Madre de Dios falls within Peruvian territory. The Indians of this river have rapidly disappeared since 1902, when the commercial invasion of the region in the interests of rubber was initiated. The following tribes, the total of whose remnants will not exceed a few hundreds, live on the Peruvian side of the international frontier.

The *Masko-Sirineiri* live between the Pilcopata and the Colorado, right-affluents ; the *Huachipairi* on the right bank of the Cōsnipata and Pilcopata ; the *Masko-Inapari* between the Tacuatimanu and the Amigo. The latter are a branch of the *Maniteneri*, of whom a further section formerly dwelt between the Purus and the sources of the Acré. These Indians are known on the Juruá as Katayana (=strong, Pano), a name applied to all relatively tall Indians of any tribe.

The *Tuyuneiri*, between the Inambari and the Colorado, are a linguistically independent group.

The *Arasa* live on the Marcapata, a left-affluent of the Inambari ; the *Atsahuaka* on the Carama, a left-affluent of the Tambopata ; the *Yamiaka* on the Yaguarmayo, a right-affluent of the Inambari. These three are Pano tribes, but in the time, at least, when they only employed their tribal languages, the first two were bilingual and also acquainted with Takana. The *Tiatinagua* or *Guarayo* of the Tambopata, who include the *Echoja* of the River Heath and the *Chunchu*, live on the Tambopata, the Heath and between these two rivers. The *Mabenaro* constitute a small group at the sources of the affluents of the Manuripe, a sub-tributary of the Beni. These tribes, now attenuated Spanish-speaking remnants, belong to the Takana family (see p. 126).

Finally, we must mention the *Amuesha*, who are semi-civilized and live near the northern Kampa territory between the rivers Pichis and Palcaza. A Romanist missionary resides among them at San Luiz de Sharon. Linguistically they must be regarded as independent.

This completes the list of the Indian tribes of Peru. The total Indian population for region (3) is

less than 40,000, of whom the vast majority are
Kampa.

Two Protestant Missions are at work in this region.
The Christian and Missionary Alliance in 1925 initiated
work among the Kampas. Their station is strategically
located at Cahuapanas, at the junction of the Apurukiali and Pichis. It is situated on the line of communication between Iquitos and Lima. The Seventh-
Day Adventist Mission has a station on the land of
the Peruvian Corporation on the upper Perené. Beyond
these two efforts, the nearest Protestant Missions are
located at Huancayo, at an altitude of 11,000 feet
on the upper Oroya, or Mantaro, where the Assemblies
of God and the Board of Foreign Missions of the
Methodist Episcopal Church of the United States
are represented ; and at Urco and Cuzco, stations of
the Evangelical Union of South America.

A Dominican convent is established at Puerto
Ocapa, near the mouth of the Perené.

The region is accessible from the same bases as are mentioned
in region (2), i.e., Lima or Iquitos. La Merced on the upper
Perené is but thirteen days' journey from New York, and
1,200 miles from Iquitos. The barrier of the Andes, however,
makes it advisable for heavy supplies to be brought via this
latter port. As has been frequently demonstrated by actual
portages, the headwaters of the Juruá, Purus, Madre de Dios
(of the system of the Madeira), and of certain affluents of the
Ucayali and Urubamba are intercommunicable.

CHAPTER VII.

BRAZIL

Area. sq. miles.	(1) Population.	(2) Indian	Percentage of (1) formed by (2).	Indian Pop. per sq. mile.
2,073,000	2,950,000	97,200	3.28	.05

Only the states of Amazonas, Pará, Maranhão, Goyaz, the Territorio do Acré and part of the state of Matto Grosso are considered as falling within the scope of this survey.

Capital: Rio de Janeiro (1,442,000). The population of the republic is 35,000,000. Government: republican under a President with a term of four years, and a Senate and Chamber of Deputies. Products: coffee, cacao, sugar, cotton, timber, rubber, nuts, diamonds and minerals. British capital invested in Brazil: £300,000,000.

For Government action on behalf of the Indians, see pp. 31–33. The Constitution guarantees complete religious liberty.

THE Protestant Churches in Brazil contain 70,000 communicant members.* A plan for national missions among the Indians has been drawn up by a sub-committee of the Brazilian Committee on Co-operation,† but nothing has yet been accomplished under this scheme. The Brazilian Baptist Churches, founded through the Foreign Mission Board of the Southern Baptist Convention (U.S.A.), have, however, recently attacked the problem, setting aside evangelists for Indian work.

---

* "World Missionary Atlas." New York, 1925. p. 77.

† For details, see "Christian Work in South America." Op. cit. Vol. I., pp. 194–5.

Roman Catholic Missions are subsidized by the Government to the extent of upwards of 115 contos (£2,875, at 1 milrei=6d.).

Although in many respects the arrangement is an inconvenient one, in order to obviate confusion we will follow the political boundaries in dividing the immense area under consideration for the purposes of more detailed discussion. Thus we have :

(1) The State of Amazonas and the Territorio do Acré. 26,000 Indians.

(2) The State of Pará. 17,200 Indians.

(3) ,, ,, Matto Grosso. 45,000 Indians.

(4) ,, ,, Goyaz. 5,000 Indians.

(5) ,, ,, Maranhão. 4,000 Indians.

(1) *The State of Amazonas and the Territorio do Acré.*[*] 200,000 Indians.

This we must sub-divide into : (*a*) The region north of the main river ; (*b*) the region south of the main river and west of the basin of the Madeira ; (*c*) the basin of the Madeira to the boundary with Pará and Matto Grosso.

(*a*) The region north of the main river.

The chief geographical feature is the valley of the River Negro. This great river finds its source in Colombian territory, while its upper waters are connected by water with the Orinoco (see pp. 12, 59). The Negro is a river of more than 1,000 miles in length, and the recipient of numerous affluents. The lower course is remarkable for its width, attaining sometimes to as much as twenty miles, while the current is sluggish and the bed is encumbered with islands. When the floods are high the panorama suggests a vast inland sea. The name refers to the murky blackness of its waters. The western affluents, the Üaupes and Isana, have been referred to in the survey of Colombia, and by far the most important tributary stream of the

---

[*] The western part of this region will be found on the map of Peru.

middle and lower Negro is the Branco, a "white" water river which rises on the boundaries of Venezuela and British Guiana and discharges its waters some 200 miles from the confluence with the Amazon. Considerable areas, both to the north and to the south of the middle and lower Negro, remain unexplored. The forest is similar to that of other regions, and is conspicuous for the uniform height of the trees along the river bank. The distinctive feature of the vegetation is the comparative absence of Hevea Brasiliensis, or true rubber tree. The quality found is known as Hevea Benthamiana, and the river is, *par excellence*, the Brazilian home of Balata gum (Mimusops balata). From Vista Alegre on the Branco north to the Venezuelan and Guianese frontiers is a considerable extent of plain, estimated at 13,500 square miles. The Negro is navigable for steamers as far as Santa Isabel, 470 miles from the mouth, and the Branco in the flood season, to Boa Vista, 345 miles from its confluence with the Negro. Above these points both rivers are interrupted by rapids, which can only be negotiated in a small launch or canoe. In order to classify the Indian tribes geographically we must further divide the region into : (i.) the western and southern affluents and the Japurá ; (ii.) the area north of the middle course and west of the River Branco ; (iii.) the area east of the River Branco to the Nhamundá, the eastern boundary of the state.

(i.) The western and southern affluents and the Japurá.

On the Lower Isana we find an extension of the Arawak tribes, whose general characteristics have been touched upon in dealing with this river as a whole. (See p. 52–53.) The first tribe encountered in an ascent from the River Negro is the *Karutana*, who are established on the left bank. Not a very powerful group, they have succumbed to processes of tribal disintegration and chiefly serve the inhabitants of the upper Negro as rowers or rubber workers. Between the *Karutana* and the *Katapolitani*, their neighbours, who are in a similar condition, the Igarapé Umaçá marks a geographical division. The *Tariana* live on the Uaupes at Ipanoré, six days' ascent from the mouth, and at Yavareté, three days further up, with a few on the lower Papuri and a sub-tribe, the Iyaine or Yurupari-tapuyo further up river. The Tariana have always played an important part in the religious festivals of the Uaupes people to the extent of being regarded as the sacerdotal tribe of the region. To-day they are rapidly adopting Tukano in place of their own Arawak dialect.

The general characteristics of the Tukano tribes have been previously described (see p. 48). The following members of this family are found in Brazil. The *Tukano*, properly so-called, are the most numerous of them all. They fall into three divisions, on the lower Uaupes to the first rapid of Ipanoré, on the Tikié and Papuri and on the small affluents of the Negro between the Caiary-Uaupes and the Curicuriary. As sub-tribes they include the Mirití-tapuyo or Neenoá ; the Arapaso or Korea on the middle Uaupes ; the Kurawa-tapuyo or Yoho-roa further up ; and the Wina-tapuyo above Yavareté. They total some 1,500. Their language, which serves as a lingua franca among all the tribes of the Uaupes, is known as Dachsea. The *Desana* or Vina have the most extensive distribution of the Uaupes Indians. They are found on the Tikié, but principally on the Papuri and its left-affluent the Macú, with some representatives on the middle Caiary-Uaupes. They total some 800.

The *Makú* deserve more detailed attention. They are roughly divided into two sections : (*a*) the Makú "mansos," or pacified Makús, and (*b*) the Makú-Guariba or " Bravos," the savage Makú. The Makú are the only tribe existing to-day in the vast territory between the River Negro, its affluent the Curicuriary and the Japurá.

(*a*) The peaceful section, also known as Nadöbo, is encountered from the sources of the River Cumapi to the sources of the Alegria or Arirahá, an affluent of the Negro, and on the Curicuriary, Marié, Teiá and Yurubaxi, affluents of the same river. On both banks of the Tikié they are fairly numerous, and between the affluents of the Uaupes, the Papuri and the Querary, they appear in even larger numbers. In these latter localities they are enslaved by the Tukano tribes. Those between the Negro and the Japurá have learned to speak the " lingua geral."

(*b*) The savage Makú or Guariba wander in the hinterland of the left bank of the Japurá from the Puré to the Cumapi. Their animosity dates from the first attempts to colonize the river. They constantly attack the settlers on the left bank of the Japurá, and expeditions of revenge have only accentuated their hostility. Neither they nor the " Makú mansos " of this

region can be numerous. Nothing has yet occurred to mitigate
the ferocity of the Makú-Guariba, and they still continue a
serious menace on the Japurá.

The Makú are a most interesting people. With the possible
exception of the Shiriana they have no parallel in tropical
South America. They are crude and primitive in the extreme.
Agriculture is unknown among them, and their nomadic life
results in their finding their sustenance in hunting, fishing
and the gathering of wild fruits. They use no hammocks and
manufacture no canoes. Their arrows are unfeathered, but
their blow-pipes by way of contrast are of skilful construction.
Miserable, naked and unkempt, their wretched condition
exposes them to the attacks and enslavement of the stronger
tribes. The tribe is bound to disappear soon as the result of
disintegration. To-day, perhaps, all groups total a few
thousands.

Linguistically, the Makú and the Puináve must be considered as forming provisionally an independent family.*
Among themselves there are wide differences of dialect, and
their range of phonetics includes many difficult sounds.

No Protestant work has ever been attempted among them.
They have visited the Romanist missions on the Papuri, but
finding it difficult to conquer their nomadic habits. they have
left within a year.

On the Mapary, a right-affluent of the Japurá, there are
thirteen families of the *Kawishana* tribe, together with a few
individuals on the Tonantins. The *Passé* are found in very
reduced numbers on the lower Içá or Putumayo. Both these
are Arawak tribes.

(ii.) The area north of the middle course and west of the
River Branco.

In this area we include the whole system of the Branco-
Uraricuera, and it is at the headwaters of the latter that we
now commence the description of the tribes. The sources of
the Uraricuera and Orinoco are found on opposite slopes of the
Serra Parima. Either side is inhabited by little-known tribes.
The Guaharibo have already been mentioned on the Venezuelan (see pp. 62), and distinct from them in the Brazilian
territory are the *Shiriana*. The latter appear to be a totally
different people from the Guaharibo, and greatly inferior to
them. Their culture is in its most immature stage of

---

* This family has been termed the " Puináve," as the name " Makú "
is applied to an independent group on the Uraricuera (see p. 95), and
to a tribe of the Sáliba family (see p. 63).

development. Their bodies are misshapen, ill-formed and dirty. Together with the Makú of the Negro, they stand among the most primitive of all the South American forest tribes. These Shiriana are not all hostile. They are found on the River Parima and upper Uraricuera and on the Motomoto near the Marutani Mountains, with a village on the Uraricapara, a left-affluent of the Uraricuera. Their imminent extinction is probable. The *Waika* are encountered in the Marutani Mountains, and they wander between the Arakasa and the Parima. On the Venezuelan side of the Serra Parima they are also reported. They are either enemies or friends of the Shiriana according to locality and tradition. Though a primitive and rude people, they have attained to a larger degree of refinement and power than the latter, whom they tend to absorb. They are allied linguistically to them, forming a group which must, at present, be regarded as independent.

The Makú live on the upper Uraricuera just below the confluence of the Arakasa. They are a friendly people on good terms with the Shiriana of the Uraricapara and the Maiongong. Every year they descend the river in January or February for the purposes of trade. They are linguistically independent, having no connection either with the Makú of the Negro or the Makú of Sáliba family (see p. 63). The Maiongong, who are Makiritarés (see p. 60), have two villages below the Makú on the Uraricuera, and are found both to the south of that river and on the Arakasa.

The *Marakaná* are enemies of the Shiriana, and feared by other tribes. They wander in the mountains to the south of the Uraricuera, and from time to time launch their attacks along the river itself. Their language is unknown.

The locality demands the mention of three Carib tribes: the *Zapara* are now mostly absorbed by the Makushi. A few live on the Island of Maracá. The *Wayumará*, reduced to-day to a few individuals, are found in the southern and eastern forests of the same fluvial island. Both these tribes formerly dwelt on the Mocajahy. The *Purukoto*, to-day decimated by disease, are encountered among other tribes such as the Makushi, Makiritaré, and the Arekuna, with a few individuals to the south of Uraricuera, a little above the Island of Maracá.

The *Pawishana*, an Arawak tribe, now very small in numbers, dwell to the north of the middle Mocajahy, a right-affluent of the River Branco. The Makushi and Wapisiana have already been referred to under British Guiana.

(iii.) The area east of the River Branco to the River Nhamundá, the eastern boundary of the state.

The principal tribe of this area is the *Jawapery*, who remain to-day in a state of uncompromising hostility. Their pacification was attempted by the Brazilian naturalist Barbosa Rodrigues, only to have much of his work subsequently undone. A state of petty warfare has continued for many years between them and the civilized communities, and their name has earned a wholesome respect along all the lower course of the Negro and Branco. The Jawapery themselves live on the upper River Jauapery, a left-affluent of the Negro and on its affluent the Alalaú. In these localities they are known as Waimiris, Krishanás, Atroahis, etc. On the Camanaú, also a left-affluent of the Negro, they are called Gabinairi, Ichú, etc., and here they harbour little animosity. They are a Carib tribe. Their number is unknown, but it is probably in excess of a thousand.

A small group of civilized *Mura* Indians are established on the right bank of the lower Urubú.

The whole of region (1) (*a*) is accessible from Manáos. Steamers from that city ascend the River Negro to Santa Isabel, and from there the rapids can be passed by canoe or launch, thus reaching the Uaupes, Isana, etc. As a secondary base above the São Gabriel rapids, São Felipe is suitable. On the River Branco, Boa Vista, a pleasant town of some 1,500 population, on the plains, and most of the year within steamer communication with Manáos, serves the same end. The Jawapery are, of all the wild tribes of the Amazon basin, the closest to Manáos. The commerce of the River Japurá is largely in a state of decay. Nevertheless, an occasional launch ascends to the Colombian frontier, above which communication is by canoe.

At the beginning of 1927 there was no Protestant mission at work among the Indians of region (1), but a party was visiting the Jawapery with a view to establishing work through the instrumentality of the Heart of Amazonia Mission (Worldwide Evangelization Crusade). Presbyterian, Baptist, Assemblies of God, and Episcopal work are represented in Manáos. The town is a base for the Heart of Amazonia Mission and a centre for the colportage work of the British and Foreign Bible Society.

The upper River Negro and its affluents, in the latter part of the 19th century, were the scene of conspicuous activity on the part of the Roman Catholic preaching orders, the results of which have long since passed away, and the wretched villages on the banks of the river are but mournful spectators of their own decay. But since 1918, the Salesians, to whom the river is allotted, have revived the work. São Gabriel has become the possessor of a school where over 200 Indian children from the Uaupes have come under instruction, and modern methods of equipment and training have been introduced. A considerable tract of land has been granted, in the upper Negro region, for the development of agricultural missions. The River Branco is under the care of the German Benedictines, whose labours centre in Boa Vista. Here they come into continual contact with the Makushi, but no regular work is done among the Indian tribes. The Japurá is allocated to the Congregation of the Holy Ghost, whose agents are established in Teffé, but apart from the occasional visit of a priest nothing has been accomplished for the Indians of the river.

The Indian Protection Service maintains a pacification post on the River Jauapery, but the Indians have hitherto shown little desire to avail themselves of the aid thus extended to them. On the upper River Branco on the plains, the Department is also at work among the Makushi.

(b) The region south of the main river and west of the basin of the Madeira.

This region has an approximate area of 325,000 square miles. It consists of low elevations and a large proportion of alluvial land, subject to annual inundations, while the forest intervening between the rivers is penetrated by numerous channels and creeks. The vegetation does not differ essentially from that encountered in other sections of the fluvial plain.

The principal rivers of this region are the Purus and Juruá. In every respect the prominent features of the one are repeated in the other. They run in huge,

G

sinuous curves which are sometimes breached in the season of rains. Each river is subjected to an annual rise varying from 40 to 50 feet. Although inferior in volume to the system of the Madeira, they enjoy the incalculable advantage of providing free navigation throughout their courses. Rapids of any consequence are absent, and from January to April, steamers drawing eight to ten feet can reach the Bolivian and Peruvian boundaries without serious difficulty. The upper reaches of these rivers are included in the Federal Territory of the Acré, which was acquired from Bolivia in 1903 by the treaty of Petropolis. The territory is characterized by superior elevation and the more frequent occurrence of hills. The proportion of land subjected to the annual overflow is decidedly less than in the lower river valley. Although distant from the Amazon itself, the lack of hindrance to steamer communication renders it, in point of fact, of easier access than many areas whose actual location appears nearer. To some who habitually associate disease with the Amazon valley, it may come as a surprise to be told that " the Acré territory is one of the most healthful of tropical climates, and persons who take elementary precautions can enjoy really robust health."*

The whole region has been thoroughly explored for wild rubber. The product of the Acré commands a reputation for value as evidenced by its higher price. The civilized population of the territory in 1920 amounted to 92,379, and several small towns ranging from a few hundreds to one or two thousand have sprung up. Such are Cruzeiro do Sul and Seabra in the basin of the Juruá, and Rio Branco and Senna Madureira on the Acré and Purus. The economic depression of the rubber industry in recent years is constantly inducing increasing numbers of the original colonists to return to their native state of Ceara. The commercial development of the region has involved the complete disintegration and disappearance of

---

* Schurz, William L., and others. " Rubber Production in the Amazon Valley." Department of Commerce, Trade Promotion Series, No. 23. Washington, 1925. 369 pp., p. 274.

many of the Indian tribes, who, in consequence, have become a totally insignificant factor in the population.

In addition to the rivers mentioned, the region covers the Teffé, Jutahy and other tributaries of the Solimões, as well as the western affluents of the Javary. Linguistically the Indians of this region belong principally to three families : the Pano, a large group, of whom the major portion has already been considered under Peru ; the Arawak ; and the Katukina. For the purposes of convenient description, we shall divide the region into : (i.) the Javary-Juruá ; (ii.) the Juruá-Tarauacá ; (iii.) the Juruá-Purus-Acré.

(i.) The Javary-Juruá.

The *Kulino* (Pano), formerly between the lower Javary and Jutahy, are to-day almost entirely incorporated into the civilized population. A few families of *Tikuna*, probably an Arawak tribe, still exist in the same region, while the *Warayku*, also Arawak, are found in a similarly reduced condition further in the interior.

It is now necessary to mention some tribes which have been grouped together under the collective name of Katukina. This family must be provisionally regarded as independent. Many have vanished in the last 100 years, and other clans are doomed to an apparently inevitable disappearance. Among them we include the following :—

The *Tukun-Diapa* live between the River das Pedras and the Itecoahy, a right-affluent of the Javary. The termination " -diapa," which frequently recurs in the names of the clans of the Katukina group, signifies "tribe." The *Ben-Diapa* are found on the right bank of the São Vicente or Cumaruhan, a left-affluent of the Juruá ; the Puku-diapa or *Tawari* together with the Wadyuparanin- and the Ururu-diapa to the west of Restauração on the Juruá. Near São Felipe are the Amena- and Kadyu-diapa. The *Parawa*, an inoffensive group, were driven across the Juruá by the Kulino and now live near the Adelia, a left-affluent, divided into two clans, the Hon- and Maro-diapa. All these are exogamic clans of the *Kanamari*, whose principal representatives wander between the Juruá, below the mouth of the Tarauacá, and the Jutahy with its affluent the Biá. The *Katukina*, properly so-called, or Pidá-diapa, are found on the Jutahy and its affluents the Mutum and the Biá, and east to the Juruá. In addition, we may mention the *Kunibo* of the upper Jutahy, of Arawak family,

now nearly extinct.   The *Marawa*, also Arawak, live on the lower
Jutahy and the Minerua, an affluent of the lower Juruá.   The
Miranya (see p. 82) are found among the civilized population
of the Solimões, on the Lake Uariny and on the Igarapé Uraua
or Caicara to the west of Teffé.

The Indians of Section (i.) perhaps attain to 3,000.

(ii.) The Juruá-Tarauacá.

The majority of the tribes of this section are Pano.   In it
we include the western affluents of the upper Juruá, and these
we will consider first.

The *Amahuaka*, whose main features have been referred
to on p. 84, are also encountered in Brazilian territory on the
Amoenya, a left-affluent of the upper Juruá, with a few survivors
in domestication between the Tejo and the Grajahu and on the
River dos Amoacas, right-affluents.   The *Remo*, with a sub-
tribe, the *Sakuya*, are met on the upper Juruá-mirim south
to the Tamaya.   The *Kuya-* or *Poya-Nawa* have been pacified
by the Indian Protection Service and grouped between the
Paraná dos Mouras and the Moa, while between the latter
river and its affluent the Sungaru, wander the miserable remnants of the *Nukuini*.   The *Nawa*, who formerly occupied the
picturesque hills where now stands the township of Cruzeiro
do Sul, have only one survivor.   In addition to these Pano
tribes, a small group of *Kampa* Indians (see p. 86) exists on
the upper Juruá-mirim, at the foot of the Contamana hills.

The Pano tribes between the Juruá and Tarauacá have
suffered no less than the others of the region through the invasion of civilization, and in addition to their natural division
into clans, have been subjected to such processes of social
disintegration that it has now become difficult to trace their
correct sub-divisions.   A feature of the progress of colonization
in the rubber-bearing forests of Brazil and Peru has been the
" Correrias," or organized hunts undertaken against the
Indians, and in this, as in other sections, the latter have succumbed in thousands to such organized and premeditated
violence. To enumerate all the clans still existing would involve
the repetition of some fifty names. We will therefore briefly refer
to the principal ones. On the right-affluents of the upper Juruá
are found survivors of the *Yaminawa*, *Shipinawa*, etc., and on
the Liberdade, the *Ararawa*. On the Gregorio, the *Kashinawa*
are united in a post of the Indian Protection Service, while five
other clans are jointly known to the whites as *Katukina*,* a

---

* These Katukina are distinct from those mentioned on p. 101.

name also applied to the groups of the Paraná do Ouro. The Tarauacá is occupied by representatives of a tribe correctly known as the *Huni-Kui*, but whose principal clan is the *Kashinawa* already referred to. They are found on the Tarauacá in domestication ; on the Murú, its affluent, to the number of thirty still organized as a tribe, but peaceful ; and on the Jordão in a savage state. This last group retains the custom of the eating their dead. The region of the upper Envira, Tarauacá, Jordão and Breo is a locality destitute of rubber trees, and, as a consequence, the remnants of several tribes, in addition to the Kashinawa, have been able to make it a refuge. Such are the *Kontanawa*, *Mainawa* and *Yaminawa*. These tribes are constantly at war with the Brazilians and Peruvians. The civilized population applies the name *Papavo* to a number of pacific groups occupying also the upper Jordão and Tarauacá, while at the Protection Post of Athenas on the Tarauacá can be found representatives of a variety of clans. The most important people of these tributaries is the *Kulino*, an Arawak tribe, who live between the lower Tarauacá and Gregorio and especially on the Eru and its affluents which are inhabited by seven clans. In section (iii.) they will be referred to again.

The total number of Indians in section (ii.) is perhaps 3,000, the savage tribes accounting only for a few hundreds.

(iii.) The Juruá-Purus-Acré.

The *Kulino*, who may be assumed to have assimilated the now vanished *Arawa*, form with the *Yamamadi* a linguistically homogeneous group stretching from the Gregorio eastwards to the Purus. They are found here on the Amaran, a right-affluent of the Tarauacá, in the hinterland of the right bank of the Juruá (including the upper Tapauá), between the Tarauacá and the Marary, in small numbers, and on the Curinaha, a left-affluent of the upper Purus. The *Yamamadi* live scattered in the forest between the Purus, the Pauhiny and the Juruá. The *Kanamari*, some of whom have been referred to in section (i.), were formerly a widely extended and numerous nation. Like most of their kinsmen of the Katukina family, they are now rapidly on the decline. They are found on the Massypira, a right-affluent of the Tarauacá, where they are known as the Wiri-diapa, and on the Jurupary east to the Pauhiny with a branch between the Tapauá and the upper Teffé. They may be allied with the *Katukina*, properly so-called, once dispersed over a vast area between the Juruá and Purus with some representatives reported recently between the upper Teffé and the Tapauá. The *Katawishi*, to within recent

times, extended from the Juruá to the western affluents of the
Madeira.   In the latter locality they are probably extinct.
Actually they may be found on the Lake Myra-pirera, about
200 miles from the mouth of the river, and on the Andira, a
right-affluent, with a few survivors on the upper Teffé.   This
completes our mention of the tribes of the Katukina family.

The valley of the Purus has been the home of a number of
Arawak tribes, most of whom, however, have succumbed to
hostile conditions.   The *Maniteneri* are a fluvial tribe, occupying
the upper Purus above the confluence of the Aracá.   The *Piro* or
Chontakiro (see p. 88) are found on the Aracá itself ; the
Kanamari between the Aracá, Yaco and Acré ; the *Wainamari*
between the upper Pauhiny and Purus.   The *Ipuriná* were
once the most celebrated tribe of the Purus.   They were visited
by representatives of the South American Missionary
Society in 1872, and permanent work was attempted among
them, but abandoned after ten years' labour.   They still number
some 2,000 or more individuals to-day, and include a number
of sub-tribes of which the most important is the *Kasharari*,
of the Curuquete, a right-affluent of the Ituxi.   The latter
river is actually the habitat of the Kangite, as the Ipuriná are
more correctly termed.   To-day they are all domesticated,
and a remarkable educative work has been accomplished
among them through the agency of the Indian Protection
Service.   Mention should also be made of the *Pammana* and
Pammari, of whom perhaps one or two survivors may be
encountered on the affluents of the lower and middle Purus.

Region 1 (*b*) is accessible by steamer from Manáos
along the great waterways already mentioned.   Towns
such as Cruzeiro do Sul and Seabra serve as secondary
bases, and the smaller affluents afford convenient
routes for launch and canoe.   In a region such as this
immense alluvial plain, it is obviously both impossible
and unnecessary to discuss all the possibilities of
approach.   A number of the rivers in the Acré territory
are intercommunicable through the forest by paths
cut for the purpose of the transport of rubber.

Though various missionary journeys by Clough,
Walkey and others have been made from time to time
on the Purus and Juruá, no Protestant work has ever
been maintained among the Indians beyond the effort
referred to among the Ipuriná.   Both the Brazilian
Baptist Church and the Assemblies of God have

members on the Purus and Acré, while a missionary of the Southern Baptist Convention has recently been working in Cruzeiro do Sul. The Indian element is of such insignificance in the region that it seems almost inevitable that nothing can be accomplished for them. There remains nothing but the melancholy contemplation of its approaching extinction or absorption into the more numerous and powerful civilized race.

The Apostolic prefecture of Teffé belongs to the Congregation of the Holy Ghost. Priests are established at Seabra and S. Felipe, but nothing has been done for the Indians, though a number, here and there, have been baptized.

The Indian Protection Service maintains posts on the Gregorio and Tarauacá in the basin of the Juruá and an encouraging work among the Ipuriná of the Purus.

(c) The basin of the Madeira to the boundary with Pará and Matto Grosso.

In area this amounts to some 200,000 square miles. The Madeira is unquestionably the greatest of the tributaries of the Amazon, and though here a secondary stream, it would be famous as the principal waterway of a continent. It is formed by the union of the Beni and Mamore, themselves the recipients of considerable subsidiary affluents, the Madre de Dios and the Guapore. The name " Madeira " is only applied to the Brazilian course of the river, the greater part of which drains the region now being considered.

The river runs through the inevitable forest, and its basin is as yet incompletely explored and defectively mapped. The zone between this river and the Tapajos is said to contain the most extensive reserves of untapped wild rubber in South America. The important tributaries, among which we may mention the Castanha-Aripuanã (Roosevelt) and the Machado (Gy-paraná), all enter on the right bank. On the left, the extent of its drainage is limited by the proximity of the Purus.

Working east from the Ucayali, it is in the basin of the Madeira that serious rapids are first encountered

encumbering free navigation and investing the traveller's journey with an added source of danger and
difficulty. The actual cataracts of the main stream
belong to the state of Matto Grosso, and will be mentioned subsequently. But on the eastern affluents
extensive out-crops of crystalline rock, which are
absent on the Purus and Juruá, give rise to rapids.
The lower flood plain is now left behind and the
rivers from this valley to the eastward are to a
greater or lesser degree characterized by dangerous
obstructions.

In dealing with the tribes of the Madeira we shall
mention first the *Mura*. This tribe once enjoyed a geographical extension approached by scarcely any other horde of
the valley of the great river. Bygone centuries found them
scattered from the borders of Peru to the Trombetas. They
were the scourge and menace of every successive adventurer
who attempted to ascend the Amazon, the apprehension and
anxiety of missions and military alike on the great Madeira
affluent, and the object of several equipped expeditions whose
operations were accompanied by the most repellent atrocities.
Harried, probably, by the persistent hostility of their enemies,
the Mundurukú, they were driven, in 1784, to seek for peace.
Since that time their history has been characterized by comparative tranquillity, although the preaching orders never
accomplished any permanent work among them. At the time
of the pacification they were estimated at 12,000 souls.

To-day the condition of the Mura reveals none of the
proclivities of the past. Many have completely abandoned
even their own language, and speak either Portuguese or, in
a few localities, the " lingua geral," submitting without resistance
to the process of assimilation. They are divided into numerous
inconsiderable sections still dispersed over a large area. Some
of these fall outside the present region, but they will all be
mentioned here. They are found on the creeks of the lower
Japurá and some of the side channels of the Solimões ; on the
right bank of the lower Urubú (see p. 96) ; on the Lake Ayapua
on the left bank of the lower Purus, where there is an important
group ; on the Autaz, a channel which runs between the
Madeira and Purus and within a day's journey from Manáos,
where there are a number of groups. Of these it is only necessary
to mention those on the River dos Yumas, who will not communicate with strangers except through a recognized intermediary.

Along the left bank of the Madeira and its affluents they are found on the Lake Arary, River Capaná, at Baetas, on the upper Acará, and on the right bank at Lake Jacaré on a left-affluent of the lower Aripuanã, on the Mataurá, and on the Manicoré, from which river some have fled to the lower Maicy. A further group dwells on the Island of Tupinambaraná. The *Pirahã* of the Maicy, a left-affluent of the Marmellos, are a sub-tribe of the Mura, with a slightly divergent dialect. They number less than 100, and are peaceful but nomadic, and extremely primitive. The *Matanawi*, also a sub-tribe, are probably to be identified with the Indians of the Machadinho, a left-affluent of the Castanha (Roosevelt). A few survivors are also encountered on the lower Marmellos. These tribes must at present be regarded as forming a separate linguistic family— the Mura. Small numbers of the *Yuma* or Arara (Carib) are found in unidentified localities between the Purus and Madeira. The *Arara* who, as enemies of the Parintintin, dwell between the Manicoré and Marmellos may perhaps be identified with this tribe. They are distinct from the *Arara* of the River Preto, a right-affluent of the Madeira above the Machado, who belong to the Chapakura family, and of whom a few individuals alone remain. The *Torá* are also adherents of this family, and are now reduced to a dozen or so pure-blooded Indians on the lower Marmellos.

Of the Tupi tribes of this region we mention first of all the *Parintintin*. This tribe has always had an unenviable notoriety in the history of the Madeira river, a notoriety due as much to the lack of reliable information concerning them as to their own unquestionably uncompromising hostility towards the white man. In 1922–3 a section of them, the Kawahib, were pacified through the agency of the Indian Protection Service, with a post on the Maicy, and in 1925 the Heart of Amazonia Mission instituted work among them on the Ipixuna, a parallel affluent of the Madeira. The Parintintin occupy an area of 8,000 square miles between the Madeira and its affluent the Marmellos. The Machado furnishes the boundary on the south. (See also p. 115.) The section here discussed falls into three subdivisions : the Kawahib on the Ipixuna and upper Maicy, the Odyahuibe from the upper Maicy to the affluents of the Marmellos, the Apairande between the Machado and upper Maicy. These latter two subdivisions are both hostile. The name "Kawahib" is, strictly speaking, the correct auto-denomination applied to all Parintintins. The tribe totals some 500. Beyond mentioning the practice of cannibalism amongst them, it is unnecessary to refer further to their customs.   A section of the Parintintin is also reported from a left-affluent of the Tapajos with its confluence a short distance above that of the São Manoel.   The *Munduruku* are found in this region on the right bank of the lower Secundury and on an upper right-affluent of this river (see also p. 109). The *Mawe*, a peaceful people who have considerable contact with civilization, dwell between the Curuauahy, a sub-tributary of the Furo de Ramos, and the Tapajos.

This completes the list of tribes for region 1 (*c*). The total population roughly approximates to 3,000.

The region is accessible by direct steamer from Manáos up the Madeira or the Autaz.   On the former river there are regular services to Porto Velho, the head of navigation and the terminus of the railway which, by circumventing the rapids, unites Bolivia and Brazil. It is a town of some 1,200 souls, with an efficient hospital, the Candelaria, in the charge of an American physician.

Although both the Baptists and the Assemblies of God have work on the Madeira, and while there are believers on the Aripuanã, the inception of Protestant effort amongst the Indians is limited to the activities indicated above amongst the Parintintin.

The Roman Catholic Church has no missions among the Indians on this river to-day.

The Indian Protection Service maintains three posts on the River Maicy for the Parintintin and Pirahã, and one on the Ipixuna.

(2) *The State of Pará.*   17,200 Indians.

It is necessary here to observe four sub-divisions :
(*a*) The region north of the River Amazon.
(*b*) The basin of the lower and middle Tapajos.
(*c*) The basin of the lower Xingú.
(*d*) The region of the lower Tocantins-Araguaya, including from the Anapú to the Gurupy.

(*a*) The region north of the River Amazon.

This region is approximately 120,000 square miles in area.   It is limited on the north by the divide with the Guianas.   The tributaries of the Amazon, of which

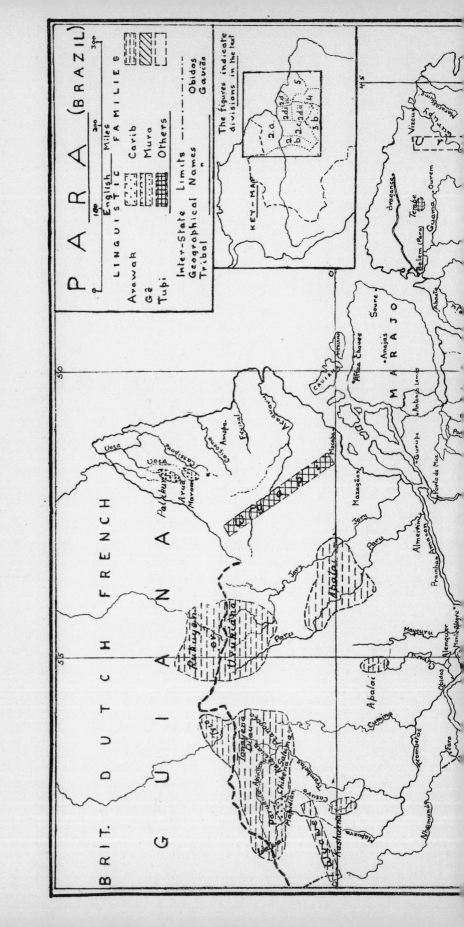

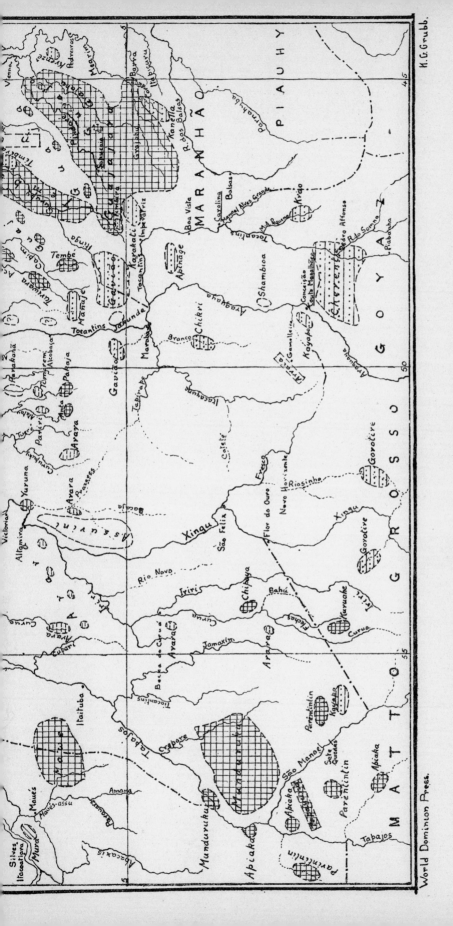

K. G. Grubb.

the principal are the Nhamundá, the Trombetas, the Parú and Jary, flow roughly north-north-west to south-south-east. In the eastern corner some small streams, of which the largest is the Araguary, reach the ocean direct. All these rivers are interrupted over the major part of their courses by numerous and dangerous rapids.

The percentage of high land in this region corresponds to that in the forests immediately to the south of the same section of the main river, and is considerably higher than in the region of the Juruá and Purus. Extensive stretches of open plain characterize the country, from which hills can generally be seen. It is said that the unexplored sector, immediately to the south of the Guianese divide, is preponderately open country, probably an extension of the plains of the River Branco, so profitably employed for the raising of cattle. The rubber industry has decayed, and the principal occupations are the growing of cacao and the gathering of Brazil nuts. The population is confined to a strip near the main river, while the Indian tribes, according to their custom, prefer the upper courses.

The following Carib tribes are encountered : The *Woyawai* or Wyawé (see p. 68) are found on the boundary with British Guiana ; on the Kafaiyana, a source-affluent of the Mapuera system ; on the Trombetas below the confluence of the Apiniwau, and on the upper Mapuera above rapids. The Indians of the Nhamundá who communicate with these would seem to be a branch of the same tribe. The *Parukutu*, probably to be identified with the Purukoto (see p. 95), who are very similar to the Wyawé, are established on the left-affluent of the upper Mapuera, on the Kaitcana, a right-affluent of the Trombetas, and on the Apiniwau. The *Chikena*, some of whom are hostile, live on the Kaitcana to the south of the Parukutu, their nearest neighbours being the *Katawian*. The *Tonayena* are installed on the same river. The *Diau* or *Yao* live on the Iliau, seven days' journey above the confluence of the Apiniwau and Trombetas. The *Salumá* are reported on the upper Trombetas and on the Cutari ; the *Pianogoto* in the source-region of the Cuminá, and the *Kashuenã* on the Casuro, or Cachorro, a right-affluent of the middle Trombetas. All of these are small tribes, some reduced to a single family. The *Urukiana*, or Rukuyen, of the Jary and Parú have already been referred to (see p. 70). The *Apalaí* occupy the middle Parú for a degree on either side of the Equator. From here they extend to the Jary and a few representatives are found on the upper Curuá (northern).*

In addition to these Carib tribes and further to the east of them we have a Tupi tribe, the *Wyapí*, or Oyampí, with a wide extension. They are found on the upper Oyapock, on the Araguary, on the Cupichy, a right-affluent of the lower Amapary, on the Maracá and on the Anauerapucú. They probably include the groups known as Kussari, Tarripi, Tamakoma and Paikipiranga. Further to the north-east are found the civilized *Palikur* (see p. 72), and remnants of the *Aruã, Maráon* and *Palikur*, Arawak tribes, and the *Galibi* (Carib) living together on the Uaça and on the affluents of the Uaça.

The Indians of region 2 (*a*) total perhaps 7,000. No Protestant or Roman Catholic work is in progress among them to-day. No Protection Posts are established in their territory.

(*b*) The basin of the lower and middle Tapajos.

The economic value of the Tapajos as a means of communication with the interior of the country is totally impaired by the numerous and perilous rapids which interrupt its course. The forest presents no features which demand comment. There is a lack of wild rubber until a distance of some fifty miles above the mouth is reached. Between the river plain and that of the Xingú extends a distinct forest-covered plateau presenting an average elevation of some 300 feet. The river is navigable for steamers to S. Luis (170 miles), a short distance above Itaituba, and at high water launches can reach the mouth of the São Manoel in about a week. The affluents in this section are the São Manoel, the Creporé, the Jamaxim and the Cupari. All these are right-bank tributaries, and all are interrupted by turbulent and dangerous rapids. It is interesting to note that the rubber seeds which were employed to initiate the vast plantations of to-day in Ceylon and the East were originally taken from the lower Tapajos. The principal town of the region is Santarem, at the mouth, a pleasant place of some 5,000 people, and a port of call for numerous steamers.

---

* Distinct from the Curuá, on p. 109.

The *Munduruku* (see also p. 106) live on the Tapajos and
between that river and its affluents the Creporé and the São
Manoel. They are a Tupi tribe, or at least have acquired that
dialect. To-day they are mostly civilized. The German Franciscans maintain a mission among them. The *Apiaká*, a
decadent and decreasing group, are met with on the left bank of
the Tapajos, below the confluence of the São Manoel and on the
right bank above that confluence. There is another section
in Matto Grosso, on a right-affluent. Their dialect is identical
with that of the Parintintin.

The Indian population of this region is perhaps about 2,000.
The only mission among them is that of the Franciscans
referred to above. The region is accessible by water from
Santarem.

(c) The basin of the Xingú.

The basin of the Xingú is essentially similar to
that of the Tapajos, with the difference that on the
Xingú the principal commercial activity is in the
region above the first rapids, while on the Tapajos it
is in the region below. The important affluents of the
river are the Iriri and its parallel confluent the Curuá
on the west, and the Bacajá and the Fresco on the
east. The Iriri and Curuá are rich in Hevea, but as a
matter of fact the population is very largely engaged in
the extraction of that quality of rubber known as caucho
(castilla ulei). The metropolis of this river at Altamira
is a prosperous place of some 1,500 inhabitants. From
Pará steamers ascend in four to five days to Victoria
(130 miles from the mouth), below the first rapids.
The Xingú here makes a peculiar bend to the south-
east, in which for 125 miles it is interrupted by impas-
sable cataracts. The neck of the bend is traversed by
two land routes, of which the better is the property
of a private trading house. This road is utilized by
motor lorries and mules, and its thirty miles of length
dispenses with 130 miles of navigation and avoids the
dreaded falls. Above Altamira navigation continues
in motor launches over numerous rapids to Flor do
Ouro, on the boundary of Matto Grosso, passing
São Felix, a small village at the mouth of the River
Fresco. The basins of the Tapajos and the Xingú are

connected by comparatively short traverses such as those between the Cupari and Iriri, and the Curuá and Jamaxim.

Between the upper Curuá and the São Manoel are two hostile tribes, the *Taipo Shishi*, probably a branch of the Parintintin, and the *Kayapo* (see p. 119). On the Igarapé das Flechas, a right-affluent of the upper Curuá, is the remnant of the *Kuruahé* (related to the Mundurukú), while further down at the confluence of the Bahú are found the *Chipaya* (related to the Yuruná), both tribes now in very reduced numbers. The *Arara*, a small Carib tribe, live in domestication on the Cupari and on the Curuá do Sul, a southern affluent of the Amazon. There are a few nomadic remnants between the Iriri-Curuá to the east, and the Cupari and Jamaxim to the west, and a group on the Bacajá. The *Assurini* are found on a left-affluent of the Bacajá. They are indomitably savage, and periodically attack the inhabitants of the Xingú. The right bank of that river is, as a consequence, depopulated for miles. They are probably not a numerous group. Their linguistic affinities are totally unknown. The *Yuruná* (Tupi), who were originally spread over the entire middle course of the Xingú, are now confined to a few families living in domestication at the mouth of the Bacajá, and a group of refugees, mingled apparently with members of other tribes, on the upper river in Matto Grosso. They were formerly famed as pilots of the rapids.

The Indians of the Xingú have suffered no less than those of other localities from contact with civilization. For many years the region was a resort for deported criminals and political refugees. Personal and business rivals obtained the assistance of the tribes in the prosecution of veritable wars. Great promises of wealth were held out to them only to expedite their massacre in thousands. Some tribes have completely disappeared while of others, only a few families remain. The Indian population may perhaps be estimated at 2,000. The region is accessible from Pará *via* Altamira, or from the Araguaya *via* the River Fresco. There is a small Presbyterian church at Altamira, but no work, either Protestant or Roman Catholic, is at present in progress among the Indians. There are no Protection Posts among them.

(*d*) The region of the lower Tocantins-Araguaya, including from the Anapu to the Gurupy.

In this region we may observe three sub-sections : (i.) From the Anapú to the Tocantins ; (ii.) the basin of the Itacayuna ; (iii.) from the Tocantins to the Gurupy.

(i.) From the Anapú to the Tocantins.

This region is characterized by the courses of a number of comparatively small affluents of the Amazon which flow approximately north and south. These are but indifferently explored. They irrigate an unhealthy region of the forest, and are all encumbered with rapids. In their upper courses they probably reach the plains which are known to exist between the Xingú and the Tocantins.

The *Arara* (see p. 110) are found in this section at the sources of the Anapú ; the *Pariri*, in small numbers on the Atatau, an affluent of the Pacajá ; and the *Timirem*, on the Camaraipy. All these are Carib tribes. The *Pakajá* are said to live between the sources of the Camaraipy and Jacunda. The *Anta* of the River Pacajá are possibly identical with a remnant of the *Anambé*, who, at the end of the 19th century, were still encountered on the lower Tocantins. Both these are Tupi tribes. The *Parakanã*, whose linguistic affiliations are totally unknown are reported from the middle Camaraipy.

The Indians of this subsection certainly do not exceed 1,000 in number.

(ii.) The basin of the Itacayuna.

The Itacayuna is the principal left-affluent of the Tocantins, having its confluence at the town of Marabá, a place with a population of about 1,000 souls and the centre of the active Brazil nut (bertholletia excelsa) industry. The lower Tocantins differs from the Tapajos and the Xingú, presenting a greater extent of flood land. It is, however, interrupted by rapids at Arumatheua 115 miles from the mouth. Steamer navigation terminates at Alcobaça, slightly below this point. From here there is a project to complete the railroad to Marabá, 450 miles from Pará. At present the extensive communication between Marabá and Alcobaça in the interests of the commercial proprietors is entirely undertaken by motor launches. The rubber industry is subordinate in this area, but Hevea Brasiliensis itself is found in decreasing quantity as far east as the Capim and even to the Gurupy.

On the Vermelho, a small left-affluent of the Itacayuna close to Marabá, a tribe of Indians has been seen from time to time. Their origin is uncertain, but I am inclined to identify them with a horde of Gavião from the next subsection. The *Chikri*, of Gê family, and related to the Kayapo, still survive on the River Branco, a right-affluent of the Itacayuna. It is conceivable that the Indians known to the civilized population as Arraia are to be identified with these.

It is possible to pass by a short traverse from the Tapirapé, a left-affluent of the Itacayuna, to the Prazeres, belonging to the system of the Xingú. The Indians of this subsection perhaps amount to 200.

(iii.) From the Tocantins to the Gurupy.

This subsection includes the tributaries of the estuary of the Amazon, such as the Moju, Acará, Capim and Guama, all debouching near the city of Belem (Pará). The Gurupy, on the other hand, flows direct into the sea on the north-east coast. It is principally a forest region. As elsewhere, the historian of the Indians of this region must wade through pages of misery and devastation. The accessibility of the locality is more apparent than real, and a profession of ignorance on the part of those who know serves to cloak the grim pageant of successive tragedies.

All the tribes of the region whose identity has been satisfactorily established belong to the Tupi or Gê families. Others, however, must remain unaffiliated for lack of data concerning them. Such are a group of Indians between the Moju and the Tocantins, while on the Jacunda, an insignificant right-affluent of the Tocantins, are reported the *Yakundá*, who are perhaps to be identified with a section of the Gavião.

The following are Tupi tribes. The *Manajé*, or Ararandewara, are met on the upper Moju and on the Ararandeua, an affluent of the Capim, and the *Turiwara* on the Acará. The *Tembé* form at present the most numerous tribe in this part of the state of Pará, and one which has figured considerably in the records of the past. To-day they are all accessible and living in peace. Including different sections they cannot total less than 2,000.

In 1919 the number of those on the Gurupy was 1,123. They
are distributed as follows. A very small group is found near
Prata, on the headwaters of the Jejú, an affluent of the Mara-
canã, a coastal river. This location places them between the
Bragança railway and the lower Guama. Here they are under
the influence of Franciscan friars located at Prata. A section
inhabits the Acará-mirim, a right-affluent of the Acará. Another
section is encountered on the Surubiu and Cauachy, source-
contributents to the Capim. Others live on the upper Guama.
The principal group is found on the Gurupy and its affluent the
Cajuapara, on which rivers they have at least ten villages. The
Guajá, who are again referred to on p. 123, are found in the state
of Pará between the Gurupy, Guama and Capim.

Of the Gê tribes we will mention the Timbira and the
Gavião. The *Timbira*, most of whom are hostile and aggressive,
are divided into different small groups scattered over widely
separated localities. The Timbira Mehí live in two villages on
the right bank of the middle Gurupy ; the Krenyẽ are known on
the extreme upper course of this river. The Krenzé are installed
in two very small villages near Bacabal on the left bank of the
lower Mearim. Representatives of the tribe are also scattered
along the Grajahu and Pindaré. The Karakatiye live between
the towns of Grajahu on the river of that name, and Imperatriz
on the Tocantins. Some of these localities fall within the state
of Maranhão, but for the sake of convenience we have grouped
them together here. All groups perhaps total 500 Indians,
or even more. The *Gavião* are also hostile. Their habitat should
be sought between the sources of the Moju, Capim and Gurupy.
" . . . At certain times in the year they appear on the banks of
the Tocantins, and will meet friendly merchants with a view
to barter, when they mass together in numbers from 200–500
savages. The day of bartering concluded, away they go to their
forest homes."[*]

The Indians of this subsection may total 5,000.

Thus for this region we arrive at a total population
of 6,200 Indians. The region is accessible by steamer,
launch and canoe from Pará. For section (ii.) Marabá
forms a convenient base. Section (iii.) can be reached
in various ways. A railway leads from Belem (Pará)
to Bragança on the coast, and thence Vizeu at the mouth
of the Gurupy is readily attainable. This river can
in turn be reached overland from the Pindaré, and

---

[*] Bland, L. In " Amazonia and Us." London, 1927. 40 pp., p. 33.

H

thus from S. Luiz.   Imperatriz on the Tocantins is
similarly a strategic point.   The Moju, Acará, Capim
and Guama are all ascended from Pará.

There is no Protestant work at present established
among the Indians of this region, although the Indians
of the Gurupy come within reach of the centre of the
Heart of Amazonia Mission at Sapucaia in the State
of Maranhão (see p. 122).   Roman Catholic missions
are confined to the contact with the Tembé referred
to above.

In addition to Pará, where five denominations
carry on, or have carried on, work, there are Protestant
believers belonging to the Assemblies of God in Marabá
and Cameta.   The latter is an important town on the
lower Tocantins, where the Baptists are also represented.   A number of believers may be found on the
agricultural colonies along the Bragança railway and
elsewhere, with a few on the rivers Acará, Capim,
Guama and Gurupy.

The Indian Protection Service has interests among
the Tembé, having established a school at Jararaca
on the Gurupy.

(3.)   *The State of Matto Grosso.*   45,000 Indians.

In spite of its geographical importance, this region
has been, at least up to recent years, one of the least
explored in South America.   Its main interest is the
presence of a vast plateau, on whose opposite slopes
rise the headwaters of the mighty systems of the
Amazon and Paraguay.   So insignificant is the sepa-
ration between these two basins that at one point
of the watershed the distance is only 310 yards.*
Arid and infertile plains of apparently illimitable extent
compose the surface of this inhospitable region.   The
rivers themselves are interrupted by rapids which in
certain localities are almost waterfalls.   The water-
courses are lined by the typical forest growth, and it
is here that we encounter the southernmost extension
of the Hevea.

---

* Between the R. Estivado, affluent of the Arinos, and an affluent
of the Tombador, a tributary of the R. Cuyabá.

But above all it is a region remarkable, in spite of all the *terra incognita* yet remaining, for the persistent efforts in exploration and pacification which will always be connected with the name of General Rondon. Although this protagonist of humanitarian activity has always had the support and resources of a Government at his back, yet his achievements would make a creditable record whatever the legitimate means by which they were obtained. Numbers of rivers have been surveyed and mapped for the first time, and, above all, the region has been opened up by the construction, with its accompanying road, of 1,000 miles of telegraph line from Cuyabá, the metropolis of the interior to São Antonio on the River Madeira. Nor has the labour of pacification of the Indians proved any the less arduous. Although even the tribes, whose initial ferocity was met with the responses of peace, have not yet wholly submitted to the clemency of a strange régime, yet the new era has been inaugurated. Officers are located at the various stations along the telegraph line and at other points, which will be mentioned in due course. Unfortunately, in spite of the most rigorous precautions, disease has already entered the pacified tribes.

For convenience in description we divide this area into two sections :

(*a*) The basins of the upper Madeira and Tapajos.

(*b*) The basins of the São Manoel and upper Xingú.

(*a*) The basins of the upper Madeira and Tapajos.*

The Tupi tribes of the region include the following : A small horde of *Kawahib* (see p. 105) and a few individuals of the *Ytangá* or Rama-rama live on the Machadinho, a left-affluent of the Machado. The *Ntogapid* or *Itogapuk*, to whom these Ytangá are related, occupy the Madeirinha, a left-affluent of the Castanha, where a Protection Post is maintained among them. The *Takwatib, Panawat, Ipotwat, Wirafed*, etc., dwell on the Riosinho, a right-affluent of the upper Machado. All

* Those who require more information on this section should refer to: Hay, Alex. Rattray, "Expedition to investigate the situation among the Indians on the Headwaters of the Amazon River between the Rivers Arinos and Madeira." *Inland South America.* 20 (1925), 23–32.

these small groups except the Ntogapid and Ytangá are a part of the Kawahib. Separated from them by the Nyambikwara nation are the *Tapayuna*, between the Juruena and River do Sangue, a hostile tribe. A few *Karipuna* (Pano) are still found near the falls of the Madeira. At the Colonia Rodolpho Miranda, an agricultural Protection Post on the upper Jamary, may be encountered survivors of the *Arikeme, Urupa* and *Jaru* (Chap-akura family) and other tribes. The *Urumi* inhabit the Taruman, a right-affluent of the Machado ; the *Kepkiriwat* the Pimenta Bueno, an upper-affluent of the same river. I am uncertain of the affiliations of these two tribes. The *Arara* (Carib) occupy the upper Guaribas, a right-affluent of the Castanha, in the vicinity of a Protection Post.

Unquestionably, however, by far the most important nation in the region is the Nyambikwara. If General Rondon's estimate of 20,000 for these Indians is correct, they must be the most numerous tribe to-day existing in Brazil. As a whole, they have adopted few of the customs of civilization. Their villages exhibit no marked progress in Indian architecture. They employ no hammocks, but sleep on the ground. They construct no canoes, but swim the rivers when occasion requires. In spite of these limitations, however, they are by no means despicable agriculturists. They plant mandioca, maize, etc., and tobacco, the excessive smoking of which is their principal vice. Although many of them are warlike, and all industrious, Hay remarks, " We found them to be genuinely friendly, and were aston-ished at the simple confidence they immediately showed in us. They are the most attractive Indians we have ever met. Mentally they are the equal of any tribe with which we are acquainted."[*]

The place of the Nyambikwara in relation to the surrounding nations and the racial movements which have affected this distant region remains somewhat of a problem. What is known of their language has not yet justified any external affiliations. The tribe is divided into multiple groups, with considerable dialectical differentiations. Such are the Nene ; the Kokozu, on the Juruena, Juhina, Papagaio, etc ; the Anunzê, grouped around the River 12 de Outobro ; the Tagnani, at the sources of the Castanha or Roosevelt ; the Waintasú, between the

---

[*] Op. cit., p. 26.

Kokozu and the affluents of the Guapore. Many others are known.

The Inland South America Missionary Union has recently established a station among them at Juruena which is manned by four workers, and the Assemblies of God of Great Britain and Ireland maintain a mission at Barão de Melgaço. No Roman Catholic order has yet commenced work amongst them.

Of the *Pareci* and *Kabixi*, related Arawak tribes, the first live scattered between the tributaries of the Juruena, and the second on the River Pume to the south of the Nyambikwara country. They have both been adversely affected by the by-products of civilization.

On the smaller affluents of the Madeira and Guapore dwell a variety of tribes, some of whom are hostile and dangerous. The *Karitiana*, possibly identical with the Pakanova, appear on the Jacy-paraná, the Mutum and the Pacas Novas. Their affiliation is unknown to me. The *Hwanyam* or Pawumwa (Chapakura family) are a timid and reduced people of the rivers Cautario and São Miguel; the *Palmella* (Carib) still survive in domestication between the S. Simão and Mequens; the *Mashubi* and *Huari*, both of whom at present must be regarded as linguistically independent, are encountered, the first on the Mequens and the second on the upper Corumbiara. The so-called *Pauserna* or *Guarayo* (Tupi) still exist between the latter river and the upper Guapore, but principally to the west of the Guapore in Bolivian territory.

This section is best accessible from Corumba and Cuyabá, but it is also reached from the River Madeira by the telegraph line track or the River Guapore. The question of communications is thoroughly discussed in the memoir referred to,* and will not be further introduced here. Details of the admirably progressive work of the Inland South America Missionary Union in the region can be found in the literature of that Mission.

(b) The basin of the São Manoel and upper Xingú.

The middle course of the São Manoel is inhabited by the *Kayabi*. They are encountered over a stretch of a 100 miles, commencing 400 miles from the sources of the Paranatinga.

---

* Hay, Alex. Rattray. Op. cit.

Their language is clearly Carib, and they appear to be a primitive and aggressive people. In his report of 1916,* Lt. Antonio Pyrineus de Sousa describes more than one occasion when he was attacked by them.   The same officer conjectures the existence of a savage section of the Tapayuna on this river, while others have reported a horde of Parintintin Indians in the neighbourhood of the rapid of Sete Quedas.   The difficulties of navigation of the São Manoel render access to this sector a laborious enterprise.

The River Xingú is formed by the confluence of at least six contributory streams, and along the banks of some of these dwell an assemblage of different tribes. Since the Protection Service has succeeded in gaining their confidence and esteem they have suffered little from the ill effects of civilization. The region is of particular interest, as in it are found representatives of the Gê group of tribes who constitute such an important factor in the tribal distribution of Eastern Brazil, as well as of the three principal linguistic families of the Amazon area, the Tupi, Carib and Arawak.

Classified according to families, these Indians are :
Carib : Bakairi, Bakairi Xinguano, Nahukwa, Yarumá.
Arawak : Meinakú, Kustenau, Waura, Yelapiti.
Tupi : Kamayura, Auyti, Manitsawá.
Gê : Kayapo, Tsuyá.
Independent : Trumai.

Some of these groups have adopted one or other of the languages of their neighbours.
The *Bakairi* are civilized and many converse in Portuguese. They live between the affluents of the Xingú and the Paranatinga. The nearest Protection Post is that of Simon Lopes. The *Xinguano* Indians are also Bakairis, many of whom prefer, however, the wild state, while some are civilized. They are found principally on the Batovy, a source-affluent of the Xingú. On the Kulisehu, another source-affluent, are the *Nahukwa, Trumai, Meinakú, Waura, Auyti, Yelapiti* and *Kamayura*. These are met at various intervals on the descent. On the Kuluene are found principally

---

* Sousa, Antonio Pyrineus de. " Exploração do Rio Paranatinga. Commissão de Linhas Telegraphicas e Estrategicas de Matto Grosso ao Amazonas." Publicação No. 34. Rio de Janeiro, 1916.

the *Nahukwa*, while further to the east on the Suyá-missú are the *Yarumá*. The *Kustenau* live between the lower Kulisehu and the Batovy. The *Tsuyá*, who are reported as a savage tribe, are encountered near the confluence of the Suyá-missú and the Xingú, and the *Manitsawá* on the left bank opposite this confluence. The *Kayapo*, a southern branch of the important tribe mentioned below (see also p. 110), occupy the sources of the Ronuro, Jatoba, Kulisehu and the circumjacent territory. Their hostility has not yet been mitigated.

Taken as a whole, the Indians of this region are industrious and active. Their houses are large and permanent structures sheltering from 50 to 300 souls. Their canoes are well made and their handiwork skilfully executed. They number perhaps 10,000.

A considerable descent of the Xingú leads to the habitat of other groups. After passing the Yuruná village referred to on p. 110, there are two sections of Gorotire or wild Kayapo. The first is on a left-affluent in Lat. 9½ S., the second on the Liberdade, a right-affluent somewhat further down. It is this latter group who extend their depredations down the Riozinho, an affluent of the River Fresco, and even cross this river to the borders of the territory of the Assurini. There is evidence that they are hostile and intractable, but the distribution and characteristics of the tribes in this region are inadequately established. The so-called Karajá of the Xingú do not exist as such. The territory of the Karajá on the Araguaya can, however, be reached with difficulty from the Xingú by ascending the Liberdade and crossing from that river to the river Tapirapé, a route employed by the Indians.

The region is accessible from Cuyabá, a mule journey thence attaining the source region of the Xingú. The Gorotire and tribes of the middle Xingú may also be found either by an ascent of the Xingú or by crossing to the River Fresco from Conceiçao do Araguaya.

No work is at present in progress among these Indians. The upper Xingú has been visited (1926) by a joint party of the Inland South America Missionary Union and the Pioneer Mission Agency. No Romanist missions are labouring here. The Indian Protection Service maintains the Post referred to among the Bakairis of the Paranatinga.

The Indians of this section may be estimated at

15,000. The Bororo Indians are not discussed in this
survey, since they belong principally to the basin of
the Paraguay. The Inland South America Missionary
Union works amongst them. Related to the Bororo
are the *Barbado*, who are found in the country west
of Diamantino.

(4)* *The State of Goyaz.* 5,000 Indians.

We include in this region the left bank and affluents
of the Araguaya, which, strictly speaking, belong to
Matto Grosso. The region is characterized by the dual
system of the Tocantins-Araguaya. These rivers
drain an area of 350,000 square miles. If it is admitted
that they form an integral part of the Amazon drainage
system, it must be conceded that they exhibit certain
notable distinctions. Their course, for example, runs
mainly in the plains and the Hevea Brasiliensis is not
found on their banks. Stock-raising is the principal
occupation of the inhabitants, while in the upper
Araguaya region considerable activity is manifested
in the diamond and precious stone industry. The
capital of the state is the town of Goyaz, from which
this area, with its commercial centre of Registro, can
be reached. In the locality of the middle river, Conceiçao, though in decline since the rubber boom, holds
the place of first importance.

In this state, as well as in Maranhão, Pará, Matto
Grosso, and elsewhere, we find further representatives
of the Gê family. Of all the leading speech families,
it is, according to Rivet,† the most artificially constituted. Nevertheless, such of its members as fall
within the limits of this survey exhibit a linguistic
homogeneity. The tribes of this family are only
encountered in eastern Brazil. Culturally their anti-
quity does not lack attestation, and precedence of
arrival in the region must be allotted to them. Even
to-day their essential differences from, for instance,
the adjoining Tupis, are clearly discernible.

* For regions (4) and (5) reference should be made to the last two
maps.

† Op. cit., p. 697.

Of these tribes we will mention the following: The *Chavante*, irreconcilably hostile, occupy the River Manso or das Mortes, a left-affluent of the Araguaya, navigable to within 200 miles of Cuyabá. Related to them are the *Cherente*, who are found along the banks of the Tocantins between Carolina and Piabanha, where they have some ten villages, and also between that river, the Rio do Somno, on the one hand, and the Araguaya on the other. In contrast to the Chavante, with whom they were originally one tribe, they are an entirely pacific and civilized people. Two domesticated villages of the *Kayapo* are situated near Conceição, where they are under the control of the priests located in that town. The *Krao*, to the number of 300, are encountered between the Rio do Somno and Manoel Alves Pequeno in the hinterland of the right bank of the Tocantins, with a few representatives possibly on the River Preto, a left-affluent of the S. Francisco. This habitat, which is not their original home, is one to which they were formerly transported by Rafael de Taggia, a Capuchin Friar. The *Apinagê* are installed in the villages of Gato Preto and Bacaba, between S. Vicente on the lower Araguaya and the Tocantins.

The *Karajá* and *Javahé* lay claim to the Island of Bananal, a fluvial island of the Araguaya. They are a peaceful and accessible people of superior stamp to the Gê tribes. An aquatic tribe, when the season permits, they camp on the beaches which line the river. Culturally they have been influenced by contact with the tribes of the Xingú. Their own language reveals slight differences in dialect between the men and women. At present they must be regarded as an independent family. A small section, correctly known as the Shambioá, are found near the hamlet of that name below Conceição.

All these tribes, with the exception of the Chavante, keep the peace with the white man, and speak some Portuguese.

The *Tapirapé*, a Tupi tribe, live to the north of the river of the same name which debouches into the western formative channel of the Island of Bananal. The *Kanoeiro*, also Tupi, are found in the hills to the south-west of the island, and have a reputation for hostility.

The biggest of these tribes is the Karajá, numbering perhaps 2,000. The total for the region possibly attains to 5,000.

Protestant missions are represented by the Evangelical Union of South America, with a station on the

Island of Bananal among the Karajá, and the Heart of Amazonia Mission at Couto de Magalhães. Believers may be met at a number of other points.

Roman Catholic orders have considerable influence, principally among the Kayapo, Apinagê and Cherente. At Conceiçao do Araguaya the French Dominicans are constituted as a "mission to the heathen."

The region is accessible (i.) from Goyaz, the capital of the State, by descending the Araguaya ; (ii.) by ascending from Marabá on the lower Tocantins ; (iii.) by crossing the country from Carolina on this latter river.

(5) *The State of Maranhão.* 4,000 Indians.

This state does not fall within the limits of the Amazon basin, but for special reasons deserves consideration here. It is a region of plain rather than forest, though the latter is far from being absent. In 1925 more than a third of the exports of the state by tonnage consisted of babassú kernels (orbignia speciosa). Cotton cultivation and cattle-raising are also the occupations of large numbers. The forest region is chiefly encountered between the Mearim and the Gurupy. The capital of the state is São Luiz, a coastal port of some 60,000 people, and from here all points of the interior are accessible by land or water. The State has considerable mineral wealth. Gold is found in the north-west, and nuggets up to 1 lb. have been reported ; gems are found a little over the border in Goyaz ; copper near Grajahu ; bauxite near the northern coast. "Some good bituminous coal is said to have come from the Gurupy."*

The *Urubú* are located between Bragança, the Gurupy and the Turyassú and in the Serra Paracambú, in which region they have at least eleven villages. They " keep far away from civilization, and are of great power, often sacking hamlets and murdering peasants. They are the scourge and terror of the Gurupy region, fighting bitterly Indian and Brazilian

---

* Shaw, E. W., Wright, W. H., and Darnell, Jas. L., Jr. " The Mineral Resources of Maranhão, Brazil." *Economic Geology*. Lancaster (U.S.A.). 20 (1925), 723–8., p. 728.

alike. . . . Europeans are said to be dwelling with them."*
Their linguistic affiliations are unknown.

The *Guajajara* are an important tribe. They are now living
in full contact with civilization, speaking Portuguese in addition
to their own Tupi dialect. They are found in some thirty-five
villages in the vicinity of Barra-do-Corda; between the Grajahu
and Mearim, and at the headwaters of these rivers; and on the
Pindaré. There is one village at the sources of the Gurupy. They
total not far short of 2,000 individuals. The *Guajá* (see p. 113)
wander in this region. Although a Tupi tribe, they have no
fixed abode, but appear at various points between the Pindaré
and the Gurupy.

The *Kanella* (Gê), to the number of 400, live in two villages
near the sources of the River Corda.

The total for this region is probably about 4,000.

Missions to the Indians are represented by one
station of the Heart of Amazonia Mission at Sapucaia
on the Pindaré, among the Guajajara. This work was
initiated in 1924 by F. Hall, an English missionary,
who died there. The same mission is represented at
Carolina on the Tocantins, whence the Kraos are
accessible. There are, in this state, a number of
believers, principally found in the vicinities of
Caxias, Barra-do-Corda, S. Antonio de Balsas,
Carolina, Imperatriz, S. Pedro, Pedreiras and Grajahu.

The Italian Capuchins have been constituted in
the state of Maranhão as a " mission to the heathen "
since 1893. Their principal centre, nearest to the
Indians, is at Barra-do-Corda.

The Indian Protection Service maintains a Post
at Gonçalves Dias on the River Pindaré.

The tribes of this state are accessible from S.
Luiz or Vizeu by water (see pp. 113–14), or from Barra-
do-Corda and Carolina by land. Grajahu is a place of
strategic importance, as are also S. Pedro and Engenho
Central.

---

* Bland, L. Op. cit.

CHAPTER VIII.

BOLIVIA

Region.	Area. sq. miles.	(1) Population.	(2) Indian Pop.	Percentage of (1) formed by (2).	Indian Pop. per sq. mile.
Andean Section ..	111,000	1,576,000	800,000	50.76	7.21
Lowland ,, ..	242,000	185,000	65,000	35.14	.27

These two entries together cover only the Departments of El Beni, La Paz, Cochabamba, Oruro, the Territorio de Colonias, and a part of the Department of Santa Cruz.

Capital : La Paz (118,000). Sucre (32,000) is the legal capital. Population of Bolivia : 2,800,000. *Government* : The President and two Vice-Presidents hold office for a term of four years. The legislature is composed of a congress with Senate and Chamber of Deputies. *Resources and products* : Tin, lead, silver, rubber, mineral oil.

A PORTION only of Bolivia comes within the Amazon basin, which covers, either wholly or in part, the Departments of La Paz, El Beni, Cochabamba and Santa Cruz. The extreme southern limits of the basin are marked by the Parapiti, but it is doubtful whether the waters of this river ever make their way to that mighty system.

All this area is drained by the great upper affluents of the Madeira, the Madre de Dios, the Beni, the Mamore and the Guapore. Until the foothills of the plateau and mountain regions are reached, there is little of prominence in the physical geography. The elevation above sea-level is slight, not exceeding 750 feet. The rivers are bordered by a low-lying strip, subject to periodic and annual inundations, while beyond this the higher land is increasingly in evidence.

The forest is neither so continuous nor of such density as that encountered in many other parts. Expansive plains extend over considerable territories, especially in north-east Bolivia, and among these we may name as of importance the Llanos de Mojos, between the Mamore and Guapore. Rubber is the principal product of the forest. For our purposes we divide the region into :

(1) West of the Mamore. 20,000 Indians.
(2) Between the Mamore and the Guapore. 45,000 Indians.

Formerly in both these regions the authority of the Roman Catholic Missions was paramount. They exerted an influence in Bolivia unparalleled elsewhere in the Amazon basin. By the end of the 17th century they had been established among the Mojo, Itonama, Kanichana, Mobima, Kayuvava, Maropa, Guarayo, Chimané and Churapa. Other tribes were subsequently reached. Except among the Kavina, Chimané, Guarayo and Yurukaré, these missions no longer exist. But their impact has left an indelible impression upon Indian life and character in the region. Of the tribes mentioned here those which show the fewest effects of such contacts are the Chama, Chakobo, Shinabu, Pakaguara, Chimané, Yurukaré and Siriono. Many of the old " missions " still exist, now unoccupied by any missionary, and a number fall outside the area under consideration. Some of these are centres for comparatively prolific Indian populations. Thus " in 1915 there were in Guarayos 6,364 Guarayo Indians, and in 1919, after the influenza epidemic, 5,607."* The Yurukaré, Chama, Siriono, Moseten and Guarayo live in uninterrupted forest land. Although in many tribes individuals may speak Spanish or Kichua, as a whole each tribe has retained its distinctive language.

---

* Nordenskiöld, Erland. " The Ethnography of South America seen from Mojos in Bolivia : Comparative Ethnological Studies " (3) Göteborg, 1924. 254 pp., p. 18.

(1) West of the River Mamore. 20,000 Indians.

The tribes here have all suffered through the depredations of civilization and a wholesale disregard of the Indian's claim to an interest and position in his ancient territory.

The *Pakaguara* are found in small numbers between the Beni, the lower Madre de Dios and the Abuna. To them, as sub-tribes, may be attached the Kapuibo on the River Biata, a right-affluent of the Beni, and the Chakobo, between the Lake Roguaguado and the Mamore. The Shinabu, probably a section of the Karipuna (see p. 116), live near the rapids of the Mamore. These are Pano tribes, but have had some contact with civilization. West of the Beni are the remnants of a people forming an independent group, the Takana. Some of them we have mentioned already (see p. 88). The remainder are sadly reduced in number and on the road to extinction or absorption into the civilized population. In the latter part of the 19th century, forty-three sub-tribes were still named. At present the *Araona* live between the Abuna and the Madre de Dios ; the *Toromona* between the Madre de Dios and Madidi ; the *Chama*, identical with the Guarayo of the Tambopata (see p. 88), in the same locality ; and the *Guakanagua* between this latter river and the Beni. On the right bank of the Beni are the *Maropa*, and further down, the *Kavina*. The individuals of these groups are principally collected in the villages of the former missions, such as Tumupasa, Ixiamas and San José, where they are nominally under the charge of the Franciscans. It is probable that the Takana family should be regarded as forming an Arawak sub-group.

The *Apolista* or Lapachu (Arawak), an industrious and civilized people of considerable number, live in the mountains to the east of Apolobamba and south of the Tuichi, a right-affluent of the Beni. South of them in the basin of the River Caca and its affluents are the *Leko*, a linguistically independent tribe. These Indians to-day speak Kichua or Spanish.

On the western affluents of the Mamore various tribes are established. The *Yurukaré* (independent) are encountered at the sources of the smaller streams which form the Securé and Chaparé, left-affluents of the Mamoré. Some of them are wild and occasionally hostile. A few are met at Covendo and 400 in San Antonio on the Chaparé, two missions directed by the Colleges for the Propagation of the Faith in La Paz and Potosí respectively. The *Moseten* (independent) are found on the divide between the Maniqui, the Securé and the Beni. To them belong the *Chimané* established from the Securé north to the Rapulo. They maintain their tribal distinctiveness, but are not hostile. The *Mojo* live for a considerable distance on both banks of the Mamoré between the confluences of the Tijami and Securé. They are an Arawak tribe, to-day all speaking Spanish. Church sums up the effect of the Mission and Spanish domination over them by remarking that " life held to their lips nothing but its dregs."* The *Mobima* (independent) inhabit the open country of the Yacumá, a left-affluent of the Mamore. The *Kayuvava* (independent) are encountered on the same bank between the Mobima and the confluence with the Guapore.

The Indians of this region number about 20,000. No Protestant work is in progress among them, though they come within the programme for advance of the Bolivian Indian Mission. The region was formerly famous for the activities of the preaching orders in the establishing of missions. To-day this work is continued on a smaller scale by various institutions. The work of the four colleges of the Propagation of the Faith at La Paz, Potosí, Tarija, and Tarata, has already been referred to, and in their missions may be met Yurukarés, Chimanés and individuals of other tribes. The Apostolic vicariat of the Beni belongs to the Spanish Franciscans who commenced operations there in 1549. The centre of the vicariat is at Trinidad (River Mamore).

(2) Between the Mamore and the Guapore. 38,000 Indians.

The *Chapakura* are found between the Rio Negro and S. Simon, affluents of the Baures or Blanco. They belong to the family of that name. The *Iten*, also of this family, formerly lived between the lower Guapore and Mamore. The *Baure* (Arawak) are established between the Machupo and the lower Itonama and near the confluence of the Baures and Negro ; the *Kanichana* (independent) between the Mamore and the sources of the Machupo ; the *Itonama* (independent), to the number of 300, at S. Ramon on the Machupo. The *Guarayo* (Tupi) are known on the upper River Blanco or Baures, and on the River San Miguel or Itonama south of Lat. 15 S. Many others are domesticated and found in such " missions " as Guarayos, Ascencion, Yaguaru, Urubicha, Yotau, S. Pablo, etc.

* Op. cit., p. 124.

The *Siriono* are wild Indians who exhibit marked hostility to strangers in their country. Though now speaking the Tupi, they hardly seem to attain to the average level of culture maintained by the tribes of this family. They wander over large tracts of country between the Guapore and the lower River Blanco ; on the right bank of the middle and upper course of this river ; on both banks of the middle Itonama and at its sources ; and from this river west to the Ivari, Rio Grande and Yapacuní. They are probably a numerous nation.

The *Chikito*, who belong largely to the basin of the Paraguay, will not for that reason be mentioned here *in extenso*. They are mostly civilized and speak Spanish to-day and are found from the Paraguay to the San Miguel with one tribe, the Churapa, numbering between 500 and 1,000, a little to the north-west of Santa Cruz. They number some 30,000 or more

No Protestant missions are working in this territory among the Indians, although it lies in the track of the further advance both of the Inland South America Missionary Union and of the South American Missionary Society. The mission of the latter Society on the Parapiti, established in 1926, falls just south of the limits of this survey. But plans for ultimate advance would cover territory as far north as Lat. 12° S. Including the Chikito, this region perhaps embraces 40,000 Indians. The Inland South America Missionary Union have initiated activities among these latter people. In the city of Santa Cruz is a mission in connection with the Christian Missions in Many Lands.

Regions (1) and (2) are accessible either by a descent of the Beni, or by a descent of the Rio Grande to the Mamore from Santa Cruz, which is within 80 miles of the head of Amazon navigation at Quatro Ojos on the River Pirai. From Santa Cruz it is 400 miles to Puerto Suarez on the Paraguay, 475 to the railhead at Embarcacion in Argentina and 300 by mule track to Cochabamba. Other approaches are either made by traversing the country from Puerto Suarez along the line of the old missions, S. José, S. Juan, S. Ignacio, etc., or by ascending the Madeira, circumventing rapids by the Madeira - Mamore railway and thus entering the navigable Bolivian

plain.   Among proposed railroad developments in
Bolivia there is a project to connect Santa Cruz and
Cochabamba, the survey of the route having been
already completed. A protocol was signed in September,
1925, between Bolivia and Brazil, with respect to the
construction of a railway from Santa Cruz to Puerto
Esperanza, which in its turn is connected by rail with
Santos on the Atlantic coast.   In December, 1926,
a law was passed authorising a passenger and mail
air service from Santa Cruz to Puerto Suarez, the
contract being given to the Lloyd Aereo Bolivianio.

Although not strictly within the scope of this
survey, it may not be out of place to refer to the
Aymaras.   If the figure quoted as 900,000 is correct
for the Indian population of Bolivia,* by far the greater
part of this must be composed of the Kichua and
Aymara.   The Aymara civilization ante-dated the
Kichua and originally enjoyed a much greater extension
to the north.   To-day they are scattered in the mountainous regions of the Andes from the Lake Titicaca
south to Lake Poopo and west to the boundary of the
republic.   Their principal divisions (see also p. 81)
are the Pakase immediately to the south of Lake
Titicaca, the Karanga between the Desaguadero and
Lake Coipasa, the Charka to the north-east of Lake
Poopo, and the Kilagua to the south. Many of them
speak Kichua, into the Bolivian form of which G.
Allan has translated some portions of Scripture
(see p. 144).   The Kichua Indians are found in the
Departments of Cochabamba, of Chuquisaca, and of
Potosí.   Among the missions who have contact with
these Indians are the Bolivian Indian Mission, the
Canadian Baptist Foreign Mission Board, and the
Seventh-Day Adventist Denomination (see p. 89).

---

* " The only point about the population of Bolivia which appears
to be agreed upon by all is that, whatever the number is—and nobody
seems to know—at least half are Indians ; and it should be added that
probably half of the remainder are half-breeds." Hill, A. J. " Report
on the Finance, Trade and Production of Bolivia." Department of
Overseas Trade. London. His Majesty's Stationery Office, 1926. 18pp.,
p. 13.

In small groups along the Desaguadero as far as Lake Coipasa are found the remnants of the Uru or Pukina, a lowland Arawak tribe.

————

This concludes our Survey of this Indian field. It may have been surprising to observe that the emphasis is given to the tribes themselves and their locations, while the references to Missions have been few and far between. The reason is evident. Among the vast majority of these tribes there is no mission work at all. Geographically, enormous territories have not even been visited by a messenger of the Gospel. Thus among the four hundred tribes already mentioned, there are only nine Missions at work in this field. Thirty-seven foreign workers inclusive of wives represent these Missions among nine tribes. The number of converts is so small that they can almost be counted on the fingers. Only the most meagre efforts at teaching the Indians to read and write are being made. So far regular school work has been found difficult. The numerical decline which goes on among these tribes makes it hard to say that the situation will improve in the future. Unless it begins to improve immediately, it will hardly be possible for it to improve at all. Indeed, it is difficult to avoid the conclusion that, taken as a whole, the Lowland Indians of Amazonia are facing sure and gradual extinction which nothing seems able to arrest.

APPENDICES

AND

INDEX

SUMMARY

Nine countries as described

Area : Andean Section, 460,000 square miles.
Lowland Section, 3,615,000 square miles.

Population : Andean Section, 4,800,000.
Lowland Section, 414,000.

Density : Indian Population, 1·28 to square mile.

Dialects and Languages : About 400.   (Gospel portions in 7.)

Missions : Nine.   *Tribes reached :* Nine.

Foreign Workers : Thirty-seven.   *Stations* (exclusive of the Guianas) : Nine.

APPENDIX I.

PRINCIPAL RIVERS

The principal tributaries of the Amazon and Orinoco are given here with their approximate lengths in English statute miles as they would be passed by a traveller descending the rivers from their sources.*

AMAZON (4,000). †

Right.

Huallaga.

Ucayali (900).
  Urubamba (550).
  Apurimac (650).

Javary (930).

Jutahy (750).

Juruá (2,040).
  Tarauacá (530).

Purus (2,100).
  Tapauá (400).
  Acre (600).

Madeira (2,150).
  Castanha-Roosevelt-Aripuanã
    (900?).
  Machado (Gy-paraná) (450).
  Mamore (950).
    Guapore (850).
  Beni (850).
    Madre de Dios (750).

Tapajos (1,200).
  São Manoel (850).

Xingú (1,200).
  Iriri.
    Curuá.
  Fresco.

Tocantins‡ (1,300).
  Itacayuna.
  Araguaya (1,300).
    Manso or Das Mortes (500).

Left.

Morona (400).
Pastaza (400).

Tigre (600).

Napo (750).

Putumayo (1,300).

Japurá (1,350).
  Apaporis.

Negro (1,250).
  Branco (350).
    Uraricuera.
  Uaupes (450).
    Isana.

Nhamunda.
Trombetas (450 ?).

Parú (400 ?).

Jary (400 ?).

---

* For navigable distances and other information see Walkey, O. R. Map of the Amazon River Plain. 1 : 1,460,000. 10 sheets. 1922.

† Measured by the Apurimac-Ucayali branch. This, in fact, is the true main stream, but in a non-geographical survey, we have retained the conventional adhesion to the Marañon, to avoid confusion.

‡ The Tocantins-Araguaya system is considered by many to be independent of the Amazon drainage area.

ORINOCO (1,500)

Right.	*Left.*
Ventuari.	Casiquiare* (225).
Caura.	Guaviare or Guayabero (810).
Caroni (800).	Iniridá.
	Vichada.
	Meta (650).
	Arauca (500).
	Apure (650).

OTHER RIVERS

The Guianas.	Colombia.	East Brazil.
Essequibo (600).	Magdalena (1,020).	Gurupy (500).
Correntyne.	Cauca (810).	Mearim (700).
Maroni.		

* The current of the Casiquiare flows from the Orinoco into the upper R. Negro.

APPENDIX II.

SOME TRIBES NUMBERING OVER 15,000

Tribe.	Family.	Locality.	Number.	Area (sq. miles) inhabited.	Density (per sq. mile).	Missions.
Goajiro	Arawak	Colombia	25,000	5,500	4.6	
Guahibo	Guahibo	Colombia	15–20,000	51,000	.39	
Umawa-Karijona	Carib	Colombia	25,000	23,000	1.1	
Witoto	Witoto	Colombia	20,000	5,100	3.9	
Jivaro	Jivaro	Ecuador	15–20,000	44,000	.45	C. and M.A., G. M.U., C.N.
Kampa	Arawak	Peru	35,000	29,000	1.2	C. and M.A., S.D.A.
Nyam-bikwara	Nyam-bikwara	Matto Grosso (Brazil)	20,000	24,000	.31	I.S.A.M.U., A.

APPENDIX III.

ROMAN CATHOLIC MISSIONS

" It shall be our principal care to extend, in these regions so vast, the field of apostolic enterprise, by instituting further missionary stations in which the Indians will find a refuge and place of safety."—Pius X. " Encyclical on the Condition of the Indians." To the Archbishops and Bishops of Latin America, 1910.

The following list only represents those missions which have been constituted for the especial purpose of reaching the lowland Indians. A catalogue of all the points at which friars or priests are in contact with the Indians would be obviously impracticable.

Republic or Colony.	Order.	Location.	Nationality of Missionaries.	Date of Initiation.
Venezuela ..	Capuchin ..	Caroni	Spanish ..	1922
British Guiana	Jesuit	B. Guiana ..	English ..	1855
Dutch ,,	Redemptorist ..	D. Guiana ..	Dutch ..	1866
Colombia ..	Capuchin ..	Caquetá	Spanish ..	1888
,, ..	,, ..	Goajira	,, ..	,,
,, ..	Carmelite ..	Urabá	Spanish ..	1919
,, ..	Recollet	Casanare ..	,, ..	1893
,, ..	Eudist	,, ...	French ..	1923
,, ..	Society of Mary	Llanos de S. Martin	Dutch ..	1903
,, ..	Immaculate Heart of Mary ..	Choco	Spanish ..	1908
,, ..	Lazarists ..	Arauca	Spanish and French ..	1916
,, ..	,, ..	Tierra Adentro ..	Spanish ..	1921
,, ..	Seminary of Burgos ..	Sinu	,, ..	1923
,, ..	St. Joseph's Soc., Mill Hill ..	Caribbean Coast	Various ..	1916
Ecuador ..	Franciscan ..	Zamora	Ecuadoreans	1897
,, ..	Jesuit	Manabi	Spanish ..	1922
,, ..	Dominican ..	Canelos and Macas	,, ..	1628
,, ..	Salesian	Mendez and Gualaquiza ..	,, ..	1895
,, ..	Holy Society of St. Joseph ..	Napo	Italian ..	1922

Republic or Colony.	Order.	Location.	Nationality of Missionaries.	Date of Initiation.
Peru	Franciscan ..	Ucayali	Peruvian ..	1631
,, ...	Augustinian Hermits	S. Leon de Amazonas	Spanish ..	1900
,, ...	Augustinian ..	' El Oriente del Peru '	Peruvian ..	1896
,, ...	Dominican ..	Urubamba and Madre de Dios	Spanish ..	1902
,, ...	Passionist ..	S. Gabriel (Marañon)	Spanish ..	1921
Brazil ..	Franciscan ..	Santarem ..	German ..	1906
,, ..	Company of the Holy Family ..	,, ...	Various ..	?
,, ..	Capuchin ..	Alto Solimões ..	Italian ..	1909
,, ..	,, ...	Maranhão ..	,, ..	1893
,, ..	Benedictine ..	R. Branco ..	Belgian, and German ..	1909
,, ..	Dominican ..	Conceição do Araguaya ..	French ..	1880
,, ..	Salesian	Registro do Araguaya ..	Various ..	1894
,, ..	,, ...	R. Negro.. ..	,, ..	1915
,, ..	Congregation of the Holy Ghost	Teffé	,, ..	1897
,, ..	Servites	Acre and Purus	Italian ..	1920
,, ..	Society of the Word of God ..	Various	German ..	1910
Bolivia* ..	Franciscan ..	Beni	Spanish and Italian ..	1549

* See also p. 127.

APPENDIX IV.

LINGUISTIC FAMILIES

I give here the linguistic classification of the tribes which have been mentioned in the body of the work, omitting extinct groups and those outside the area discussed. The name of each family is given in capital letters, and where no further names are appended it may be assumed that the family consists only of the tribe bearing that name.

I. AMUESHA.

II. ARAWAK.
- Achagua.
- Adzaneni (Tatú-tapuyo).
- Amarizama.
- Apolista (Lapachu).
- **Arawak.**
- Baniwa.
- Barawana.
- Baré.
- Baure.
- Chukuna.
- Goajiro.
    - Epieyue, Kosina, Uriana, Parauhano, etc.
- Guinau.
- Huachipairi.
- Huhuteni.
- Ipeka (Kumatá-minanei).
- Ipuriná (Kangite).
    - Kasharari.
- Kabixi.
- Kampa (Anti).
    - Kamatika, Katongo, Kimbiri, Kimiairi, Macheyenga (Mesheringa), Pangoa, Pukapakuri, Unini, Ungonino, etc.
- Kanamari.
- Karutana.
- Katapolitani.
- Kauyari (Wainamby-tapuyo).

II. ARAWAK—*continued*.
- Kawa.
- Kawishana.
- Kuati (Kapiti-minanei).
- Kulino.
    - Arawa.
- Kunibo.
- Kushiteneri.
- Kustenau.
- Mandawaka.
- Maniteneri.
- Masko-Inapari (Katayana).
- Mapidian.
- Maráon.
- Marawa.
- Masko-Sirineiri.
- Matapy.
- Mawaka.
- Meinakú.
- Mitua.
- Mojo.
- Palikur.
- Pammana.
- Pammari.
- Pareci.
- Passé.
- Pawishana.
- Payoarini.
- Piapoko.
- Piro (Chontakiro).
- Siusi (Oalíperi-dakeni).
    - Moliweni.
- Tamude.
- Tapiira.

Note.—Portions of scripture have been published in those languages printed in bold type, see p. 143, Appendix V.

II. ARAWAK—*continued.*

Tariana.
Iyäine (Yurupari-
   tapuyo).
Taruma.
Tereno.
Tikuna.
Uru (Pukina).
Wainamari.
Wapisiana.
   Atorai.
Warekena.
Warayku.
Waura.
Yabaana.
Yamamadi.
Yavitero.
Yukuna.

III. ARRAIA.*

IV. ASSURINI.*

V. AWAKE.

VI. AYMARA.

VII. BORORO.

Bororo.
Barbado.

VIII. CARIB.

Akawai (Waika).
Akuria.
Apalaí.
Arara.
Arekuna (Jarikuna).
Bakairi.
   Xinguano.
Chakoi.
Jawapery.
   Atroahi,   Gabinairi,
   Ichú,   Krishaná,
   Waimiri, etc.
Kaliña (Galibi, Karaib).
Karib.
Kariniako.
Kashuenä.
Katawian.
Kayabi.
Kirikiripa.
Kumayena.

VIII. CARIB—*continued.*

Kurasikana.
Makiritare (Maiongong,
   Waiomgomo).
Makushi.
Mapoyo.
Motilon.
   Apon, Aponcito, Chaké,
   Chaparro,   Irapeno,
   Makoa,   Pariri,   Rio
   Negro, Tukuku, Yasa,
   Yukuri, etc.
Nahukwa.
Palmella.
Panare.
Pariri.
Partamona.
Peba.
Pianagoto.
Purukoto (Parukutu).
Rukuyen (Oyana, Uru-
   kiana, Urukuena).
   Upurui.
Salumá.
Seregong.
Taira.
Taparito.
Timirem.
Tonayena.
Trio.
Umawa-Karijona.
   Guake,   Hianakoto,
   Kahätonari,   Kaikut-
   shana,   Karijona,
   Mahotoyana, Tsahát-
   saha, Yakaoyana, etc.
Vökiare.
Wayumará.
Wyawé (Wai-wai, **Woya-**
Yabarana.   **[wai].**
Yagua.
Yameo.
Yao (Diau).
Yaruma.
Yuma.
Zapara.

IX. CHAPAKURA.

Arara.
Arikeme.
Hwanyam (Pawumwa).
Jaru.
Torá.
Urupa.

---

* These tribes are allotted an independent place owing to the lack of satisfactory data for their classification.

NOTE.—Portions of scripture have been published in those languages
printed in bold type, see p. 143, Appendix V.

X. CHIBCHA.

Andaki.
Aruak.
    Atankez, Bintukua,
    Guamaka, Kágaba.
Chimila.
Guatuso.
Kayapa.
Kolorado.
Kwaiker.
Paez.
    Guanaka, Kokonuko,
    Moguex, Totoro.
Panikita.
Tairona.
Telembi.
Tunebo.
    Pedraza, etc.
Yumbo.

XI. CHIKITO.

Chikito.
Churapa.

XII. CHOKO.

Etc.

XIII. GÊ.

Apinagê.
Chavante.
Cherente.
Chikri.
Gavião.
    Yakundá.
Kanella.
Kayapo.
    Gorotire.
Krao.
Timbira.
    Karakatiye, Krenyĕ,
    Krenzé, Mehí.
Tsuyá.

XIV. GUAHARIBO.*

XV. GUAHIBO.

Guahibo.
Chirikoa.
Churroya.
Katarro.

XV. GUAHIBO—*continued*.

Kuiloto.
Kuiva (Mella, Ptamo).
Yamu.

XVI. HIBITO.

Hibito.
Cholona.

XVII. HUARI.

XVIII. ITONAMA.

XIX. JIRAJARA.

Ajagua.
Ayaman.
Gayon.
Jirajara.

XX. JIVARO.

Achuale.
Aguaruna.
Alapiko.
Antipa.
Cherembo.
Chiguasa.
Chihuando.
Chirapa.
Gualaquiza.
Huambisa.
Huamboya.
Indanza.
Jivaro.
Kandoashi.
Kangaime.
Kapahuari.
Kopatasa.
Machine.
Mangosisa.
Morona.
Murato.
Naranza.
Palora.
Pastaza.
Pindu.
Santiago.
    Iransa, Patokuma.
Yunganza.
Zamora.
Etc.

---

* This tribe is allotted an independent place owing to the lack of satisfactory data for its classification.

XXI. KALIANA.

XXII. KANICHANA.

XXIII. KARAJA.

Javahé.
Karajá.
Shambioá.

XXIV. KARITIANA.

XXV. KATUKINA.

Kanamari.
Amena-diapa, Ben-diapa, Kadyu-diapa, Parawa.
Hon-diapa, Maro-diapa.
Pida-diapa, Tawari (Puku-diapa), Tukun-diapa, Ururu-diapa, Wadyu-paranin-diapa, Wiri-diapa.
Katawishi.
Katukina.

XXVI. KAYUVAVA.

XXVII. KEPKIRIWAT.

XXVIII. KICHUA.

XXIX. LEKO.

XXX. MÁKU.

XXXI. MASHUBI.

XXXII. MIRANYA (Boro).

XXXIII. MOBIMA.

XXXIV. MOKOA.

XXXV. MOSETEN.

Moseten.
Chimané.

XXXVI. MURA.

Mura.
Matanawi.
Pirahã.

XXXVII. NYAMBIKWARA.

Anunzê.
Kokozu.
Nene.
Tagnani.
Waintasú.
Etc.

XXXVIII. PAKANOVA.*

XXXIX. PANO.

Amahuaka.
Espino.
Arasa.†
Atsahuaka.†
Huni-kui.
Kashinawa, Katukina etc.
Kapanawa.
Karipuna.
Shinabu.
Kashibo.
Konibo.
Kontanawa.
Kulino.
Kuyanawa.
Mainawa.
Mayoruna (Mayo).
Marubo, Pisabu.
Nawa.
Nukuini.
Pakaguara.
Chakobo, Kapuibo.
Papavo.
Poyanawa.
Remo.
Mananagua, Sakuya.
Sensi.
Shetebo.
Shipibo.
Sinabu.
Shipinawa.
Yamiaka.†
Yaminawa.

---

* This tribe is allotted an independent place owing to the lack of satisfactory data for its classification.

† See p. 88.

NOTE.—Portions of scriptures have been published in those languages printed in bold type, see p. 143, Appendix V.

XL. PARAKANÃ.*

XLI. PUINAVE.

Makú.
Makú-Guariba.
Nadöbo.
Puináve (Epined).

XLII. SALIBA.

Máku.
Piaroa.
Sáliba.

XLIII. SHIRIANA.

Waika.

XLIV. TAKANA.

Araona.
Chama.
Guakanagua.
Kavina.
Mabenaro.
Maropa.
Tiatinagua.
  Chunchu.
  Echoja.
  Guarayo.
Toromona.

XLV. TRUMAI.

XLVI. TUKANO.

Abijira (Avishiri).
Airiko.
Bará.
Bariguda.
Buhágana.
  Etc.
Desana (Vina).
Diria.
Enkabellado.
Hölöwa (Baniwa, Yulä-
  mawa).
Karapaná.
Kawiria.
Kobewa.
  Bahuna, Koroa, etc.

XLVI. TUKANO—*continued.*

Koreguaje.
Kueretu.
Makaguaje.
Opaina.
  Letuana (Retuana).
  Tanimuka.
Pamoa.
Pioje.
Siglia.
Siona.
Tama.
Tukana.
  Arapaso, Korea, Nee-
  noá (Miriti-tapuyo),
  Wina-tapuyo, Yohoroa
  (Kurawa-tapuyo).
Tuyuka (Doghapura).
Waikana.
Waínana.
Wanána.
Yabahana.
Yupua.

XLVII. TUPI-GUARANI.

Anambé (Anta).
Apiaka.
Auyti.
Chipaya.
Emerillon.
Guajá.
Guajajara.
Guarani.
Guarayo (Pauserna).
Itogapuk (Ntogapid).
Kamayura.
Kanoeiro.
Kokama.
Kokamilla.
Kuruahé.
Manajé.
Manitsawa.
Mawe.
Mundurukú.
Omagua.
Pakajá.
Parintintin.
  Apairande, Ipotwat,
  Kawahib, Odyahuibe,
  Panawat, Taipo Shishi,
  Takwatib, Wirafed.
Rama-rama.
Siriono.
Tapayuna.

---

* This tribe is allotted an independent place owing to the lack of satisfactory data for its classification.

NOTE.—Portions of scripture have been published in those languages printed in bold type, see p. 143, Appendix V.

XLVII. TUPI-GUARANI
continued.
    Tapirapé.
    Tembé.
    Turiwara.
    Wyapí (Oyampi).
      Kussari, Paikipiranga,
      Tamakoma, Tarripi,
      Yelapiti.
    Ytangá.
    Yuruná.

XLVIII. TUYUNEIRI.

L. URUBÚ.*

LI. URUMI.*

LII. YARURO.

LIII. YURI.

LIV. YURUKARÉ.

LV. WARAU (Guarauno).

LVI. WITOTO.
    Orejone.
    Witoto.

LVII. ZAPARO.
    Andoa.
    Auka.
    Kuraraye.
    Nushino.
    Pinche.
    Supinu.
    Yasuni.
    Zaparo.
    Etc.

---

* These tribes are allotted an independent place owing to the lack of satisfactory data for their classification.

NOTE.—Portions of scripture have been published in those languages printed in bold type. see p. 143, Appendix V.

APPENDIX V.

Bible Translations

Tribe.	Location.	Linguistic Family.	Portion.	Date.	Publisher.	Translator.
Karib	Honduras	Carib	Matthew	1847	T. Constable	A. Henderson.
,,	,,	,,	Mark *	1896	B.F.B.S. ..	J. F. Laughton.
,,	,,	,,	John ..	1902	,,	,,
Akawai	B.Guiana	,,	Selections	1873	S.P.C.K. ..	W. H. Brett.
Makushi	,,	,,	John ..	1923	B.F.B.S. ..	W. G. White.
Arawak	Guiana	Arawak	Selections	1799	C. Cist. ..	J. J. G. Fischer.
,,	,,	,,	Matt. and John	1850	S.P.C.K. ..	W. H. Brett.
,,	,,	,,	Acts	1850	A.B.S. ..	T. Schultz.
,,	,,	,,	Selections, Gosps. & Acts ..	1856	S.P.C.K. ..	W. H. Brett.
Warau	,,	Warau	,,	1850	S.P.C.K. ..	
Kichua	Peru ..	Kichua	John†	1880	B.F.B.S. ..	T. H. Gybbon-Spilsbury.
,,	,, ..	,,	Luke ..	1901	A.B.S. ..	C. M. de Turner.
,,	,, ..	,,	Acts ..	1901	,, ..	,,
,,	,, ..	,,	John ..	1901	,, ..	,,
,,	,, ..	,,	Romans	1901	,, ..	,,
,,	,, ..	,,	Mark ..	1903	,, ..	,,
,,	,, ..	,,	Matthew	1904	,, ..	,,
,,	,,	,,	Luke‡ ..	1912	,, ..	T. R. Wood.
,,	Huanuco (Peru)	,,	Selections	Not dated	" El Inca "	T. W. Smith.
,,	,,	,,	Matthew	1917	S.G.M. ..	L. Chocano and T. W. Smith.
,,	,,	,,	Gospels	1923	B.F.B.S. ..	,,
,,	Ecuador	,,	Luke ..	1917	A.B.S. and B.F.B.S.	J. D. Woodward.
,,	Bolivia	,,	John§ ..	1907	A.B.S. and others	G. Allan.
,,	,,	,,	Matthew	1917	A.B.S. and B.F.B.S.	,,
,,	,,	,,	Mark ..	1917	,, ..	,,
,,	,,	,,	Luke ..	1917	,, ..	,,
,,	,,	,,	John ..	1917	,, ..	,,
,,	,,	,,	Gospels‖	1917	,, ..	,,
,,	,,	,,	N.T. ..	1922	,, ..	,,
Aymara	,,	Aymara	Luke ..	1829¶	B.F.B.S. ..	V. P. Kanki.
Guarani	Paraguay	Tupi	Selections	1888	,, ..	W. Stewart.
,,	,,	,,	Luke ..	1905	,, ..	J. W. Lindsay.
,,	,,	,,	Acts ..	1907	,, ..	,,
,,	,,	,,	N.T. ..	1913	,, ..	,,
,,	,,	,,	Luke**	1914	,, ..	,,
,,	,,	,,	Acts ..	1914	,, ..	,,

* Reprinted in 1901.　　　† Reprinted in 1897.
‡ A revision of (12).　　　§ A revision of (14).
‖ Nos. 24–27 bound together.　¶ Reproduced again in 1898 and 1910.
** Reprinted from (34).

INDEX

Names of Indian Tribes, Groups, etc., are in *italics*.

K